Microsoft Dynamics CRM 4.0 Online

Quick Reference

Edward Kachinske

Timothy Kachinske

Adam Kachinske

About the Authors

Edward Kachinske has written more than 25 books on CRM-related topics, including Maximizing Your Sales with Microsoft Dynamics CRM, Maximizing Your Sales with Salesforce.com, Managing Contacts with Outlook, the Official ACT! Course Manuals for Instructor-Led Training, and more. He is a frequent speaker at CRM-related conferences and is on the Microsoft Dynamics EC Advisory Board.

Edward is the President of Innovative Solutions, a Gold Certified Microsoft Dynamics CRM Partner. Innovative Solutions is a Microsoft Dynamics President's Club member, ranking in the top 5% for sales of Microsoft Dynamics CRM worldwide. Edward is certified in Microsoft Dynamics CRM and is a Microsoft Certified Trainer. He holds a dozen other Microsoft certifications, including the Microsoft Certified IT Professional status.

Timothy Kachinske has written more than a dozen books on CRM and non-profit management topics. Titles written by Tim include Maximizing Your Sales with Microsoft Dynamics CRM, Maximizing Your Sales with Salesforce.com, 90 Days to Success in Fundraising, and 90 Days to Success in Grant Writing. He has 17 years of experience as a development officer for various non-profit organizations, and has been designing CRM solutions for NFP organizations for more than a decade.

Tim teaches an online class on Microsoft Dynamics CRM and a class on non-profit fundraising through a consortium of colleges and universities. Through this consortium, Tim's classes are distributed to more than 1,500 colleges and universities in North America. Tim is a Microsoft Certified Trainer and is certified in Microsoft Dynamics CRM and Sharepoint.

Adam Kachinske is a CRM consultant for Innovative Solutions in Washington, DC. In addition to this book, Adam is an author of Maximizing Your Sales with Microsoft Dynamics CRM 2011 and the Innovative Solutions set of Microsoft Dynamics CRM Quick Reference Cards. He is a Microsoft Certified Technical Specialist for Microsoft Dynamics CRM and Sharepoint.

Table of Contents

CHAPTER

1

Ready... Set... CRM Online!

Signing up for a CRM Online trial ◆ Obtaining a Windows Live ID ◆ Logging into Microsoft Dynamics CRM Online ◆ Activating your trial to a paid subscription

Signing up for a CRM Online Trial

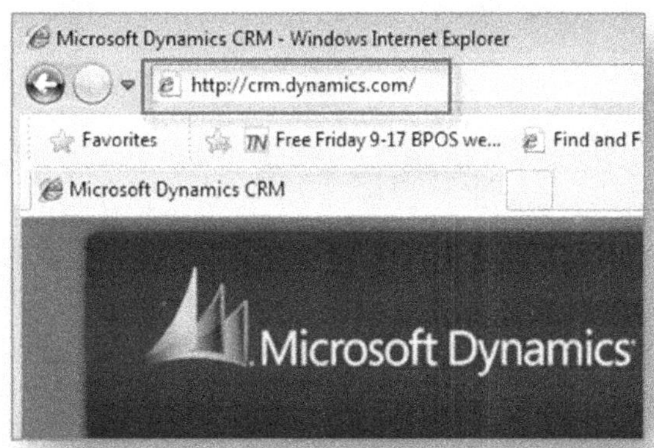

You'd probably be disappointed if you bought Microsoft Dynamics CRM Online only to find out that you didn't like it. This is why Microsoft offers you a free thirty day trial of Dynamics CRM Online.

This trial will give you the chance to fool around with Microsoft Dynamics CRM and decide whether or not you want to buy it. you can upgrade to a paid subscription at any time over the course of the trial period. If you don't upgrade you will lose your data.

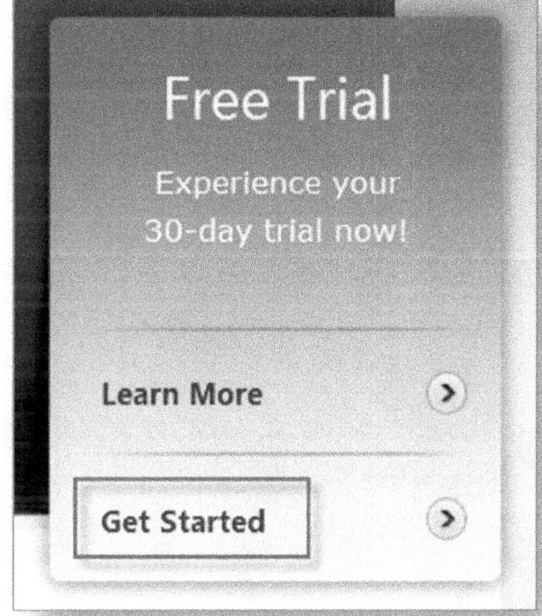

Step-by-Step Instructions

1. In Internet Explorer (not Firefox) go to http://crm.dynamics.com.
2. Click on the Getting Started button under the Free Trial header.
3. Select your country and click Submit.
4. Enter the required information to activate your trial.

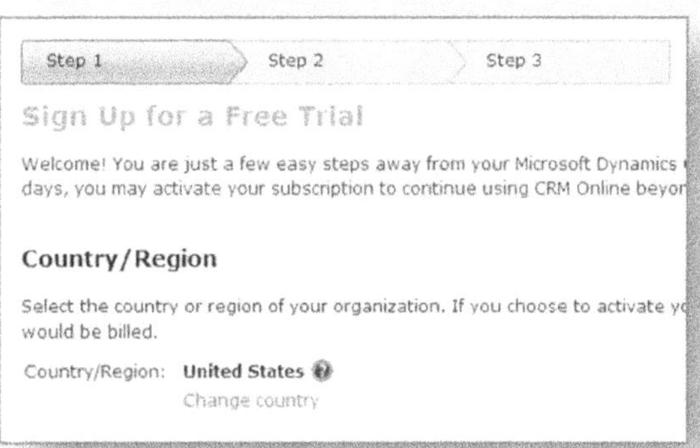

Tips & Tricks

- Trials last for thirty days.
- At the end of thirty days, you can sign up for another trial, but none of your data would come over into the new trial database.

Obtaining a Windows Live ID

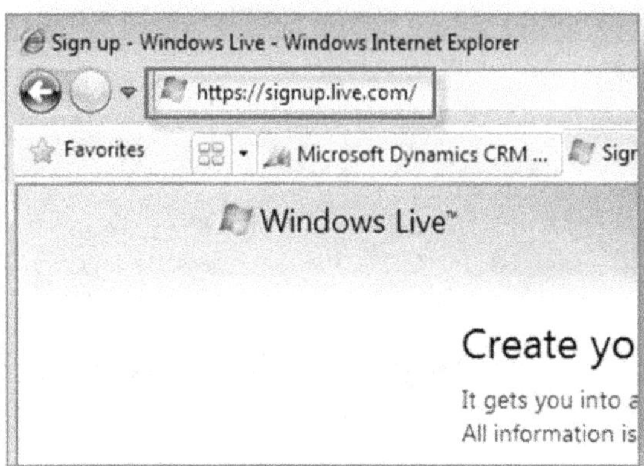

If you use **Hotmail**, **Messenger**, or **Xbox LIVE**, you already have a Windows Live ID. Sign in

Use your email address: Example: someone@example.com

Or get a Windows Live email address

Create a password:

6-character minimum; case sensitive

Retype password:

First name:

Last name:

Country/region: United States

State: Select one

ZIP code:

You'll need a Windows live ID before you can do anything in Microsoft Dynamics CRM Online. Fortunately, you don't have to pay a dime for a Windows Live ID, and it can be used to log into other Microsoft websites - like Bing, Zune, Xbox, etc.

Step-by-Step Instructions

1. Type https://signup.live.com in the address bar of Internet Explorer. (Don't forget the "s" in https.)
2. Enter in the required information.
3. Click I Accept.

Tips & Tricks

- If you have a Hotmail account, you can link your Hotmail account to another Windows Live ID. Once you sign up for a Windows Live ID using your business e-mail address, you'll have an option to link the accounts. Then, if you're logged into your business Windows Live ID, you won't have to log out to check your personal Hotmail e-mail.
- If you have many users running Microsoft Dynamics CRM Online, you should ask your consultant or Microsoft rep about options for creating multiple Windows Live IDs. By default, you can only create 3 per IP address per day.

Logging into CRM Online

Microsoft Dynamics CRM Online is a web-based application, which means that you don't need to install any software on your computer. No more CDs, no more lost serial keys, and no more installing software! Instead, the application runs in Microsoft Internet Explorer or as a lightweight plugin in Outlook.

Microsoft Dynamics CRM Online will only work on a computer running Microsoft Windows XP SP2 or better. Microsoft Internet Explorer 6.0 SP2 or higher is also required. And if you're still using Outlook 2002 or older, climb out from under your rock, install Outlook 2003+, and try again.

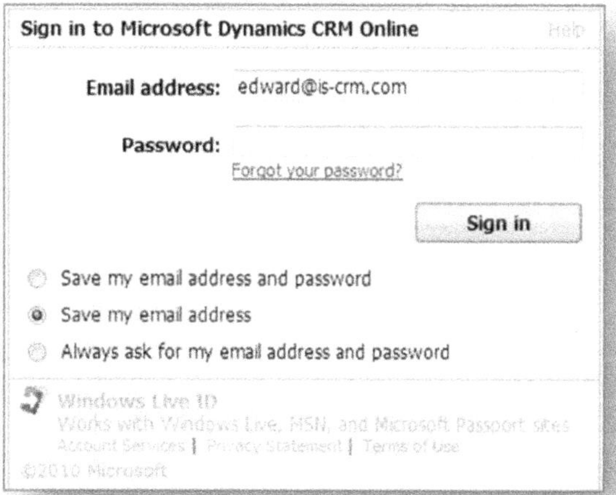

Step-by-Step Instructions

1. Go directly to https://yourname.dynamics.com. Substitute yourname for your organization's database name. Ask your administrator if you unsure of the URL name.

2. Enter your Windows Live e-mail address and password. Click Sign In.

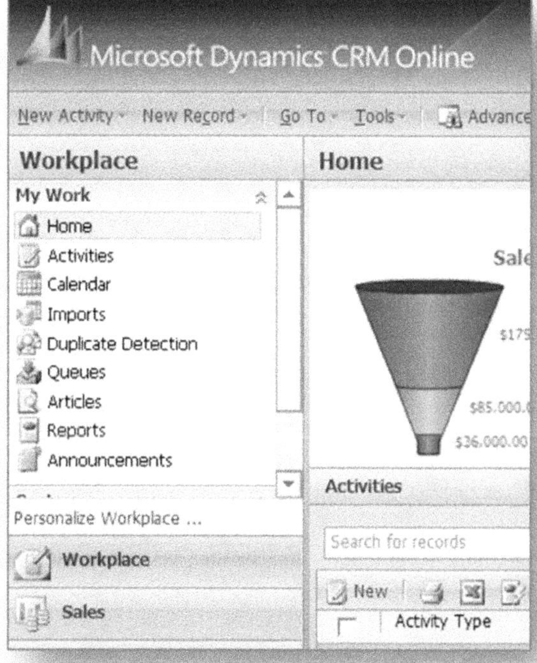

Tips & Tricks

- Choose the Remember Password if you don't want to type your password every time you log in.

- Go to this web site to reset your Windows Live ID if you've forgotten it: account.live.com/ResetPassword.aspx

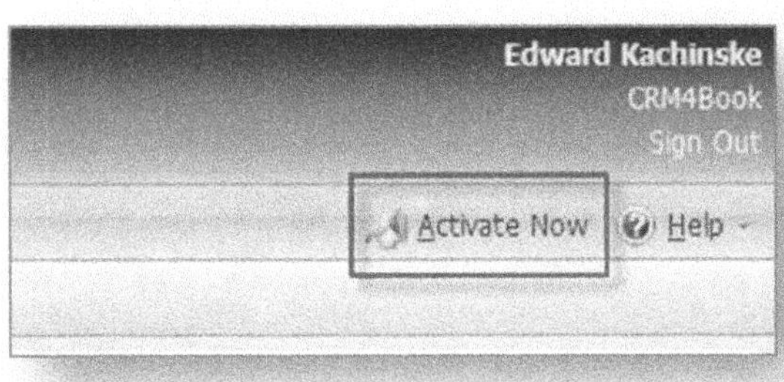

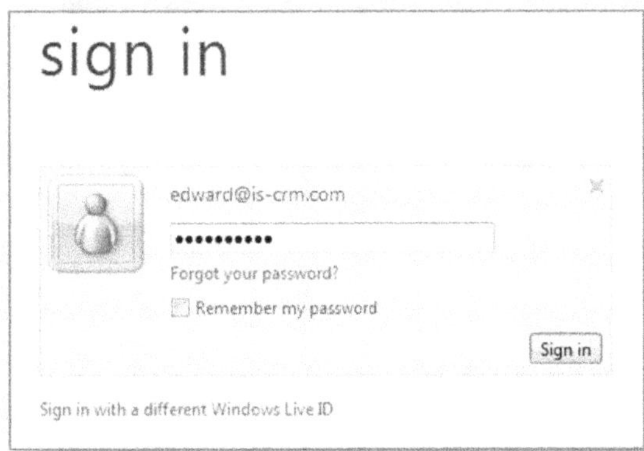

Activating your trial to a paid subscription

You can't get away with using the free trial of Microsoft Dynamics CRM forever, so at some point during the thirty days you will want to activate to a paid subscription.

Don't worry about any of the data in your trial subscription - it will still be in the same spot once you activate the paid subscription. If you don't activate, all of your data will be lost after 30 days.

Step-by-Step Instructions

1. In Microsoft Dynamics CRM Online, click Activate Now on the application menu toolbar.

2. Enter your Windows Live e-mail address and password.

3. Enter the required information to activate your account. (Have your credit card handy.)

Tips & Tricks

- Only the person who originally signed up for the trial will be able to activate.

- Call 877-CRM-CHOICE, option 2 if you need help activating.

You mean I never have to leave Outlook?

Installing the Outlook plug-in ◆ Updating the plugin to the latest build ◆ Setting favorites for commonly used CRM entities ◆ Specifying which contacts sync down to Outlook ◆ Forcing a synchronization ◆ Working offline ◆ Sending contacts from Outlook to CRM ◆ Tracking e-mails in CRM ◆ Tracking appointments and tasks in CRM

Installing the Outlook plug-in

You always have Outlook open. If you don't, you're probably not working anyway. One of the greatest features of Microsoft Dynamics CRM is that you can access all of your data directly within Outlook. There isn't another button to click. There aren't other windows to open. If you have e-mail up, you also have your database open.

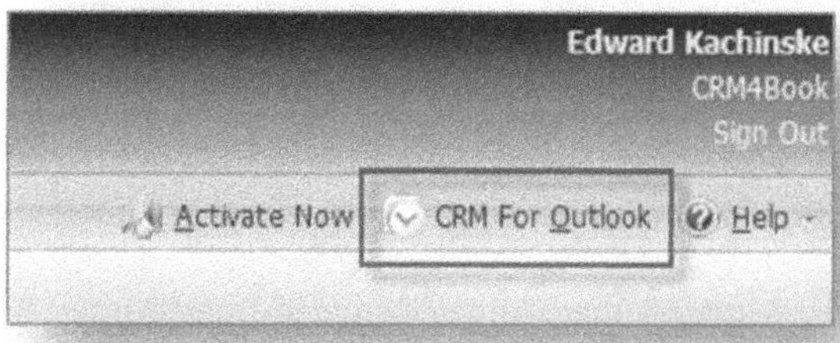

If you are familiar with Outlook, then getting used to Microsoft Dynamics CRM for Outlook should be a cinch.

Step-by-Step Instructions

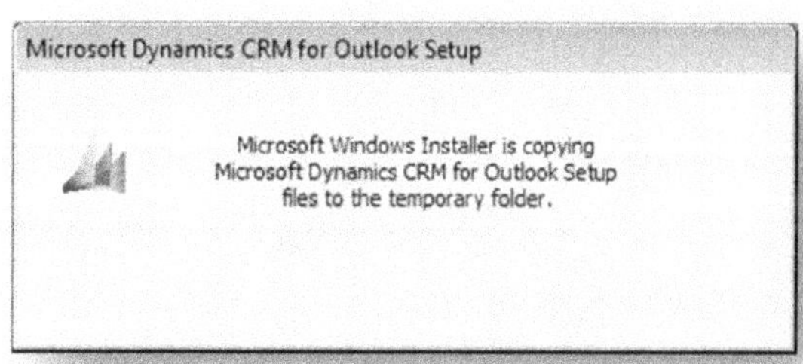

1. On a computer that doesn't have the Outlook plug-in installed, log into your Microsoft Dynamics CRM database by going to **yoursite.crm.dynamics.com** in Internet Explorer.

2. Click the CRM for Outlook button on the toolbar.

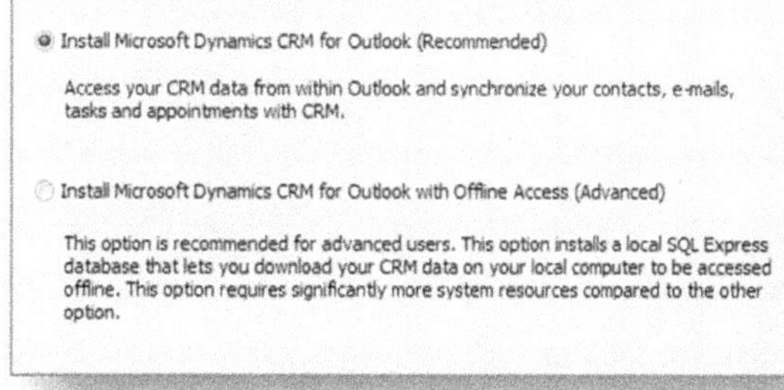

3. Run the client installer when prompted.

Tips & Tricks

- If in doubt, choose the option to install *without* offline access. Installing the Outlook plug-in will install a local instance of MS SQL Server and slow your computer down big time.

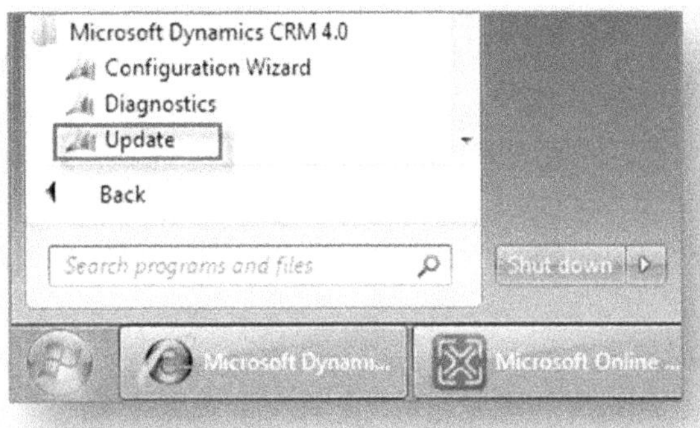

Updating the plug-in to the latest build

Did your computer freeze? Before you swear off technology completely, update Microsoft Dynamics CRM to the latest build. This will make sure that you have the latest version of the product with the newest bug-fixes and features.

Making sure you are on the latest build of the Microsoft Dynamics CRM plugin is the best way to ensure that you have the smoothest possible experience. (And it's cheaper than hiring someone to figure out why CRM isn't working with your latest service pack of Office.)

Step-by-Step Instructions

1. Click Start | All Programs | CRM 4.0 | Update.
2. Follow the steps to update the plug-in.

Tips & Tricks

- You'll need to be connected to the Internet to perform an update.
- If you already have the latest build of the software, the update will let you know that everything is up-to-date.

Setting favorites for commonly used CRM entities

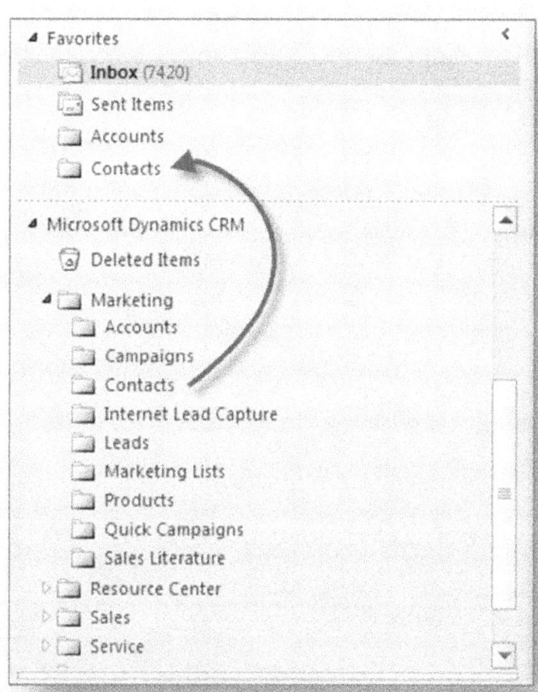

Commonly used CRM entities can be dragged into your Outlook Favorites area. This means that you can spend less time scrolling up and down through different folders and more time being productive.

It's time to start putting your contacts, opportunities, and secrets into Microsoft Dynamics CRM. It's actually a lot easier than you might think...because everything important will be just a single click away.

Step-by-Step Instructions

1. Locate your favorite CRM entity, like Contacts or Opportunities. You'll find the entities hidden in an area marked Microsoft Dynamics CRM under your Inbox in the Mail section of Outlook.

2. Drag any CRM entity, such as Contacts, up into the Favorites section of Outlook.

Tips & Tricks

- Anything added to your Favorites section in Outlook will only affect you. Other network users have their own Favorites.

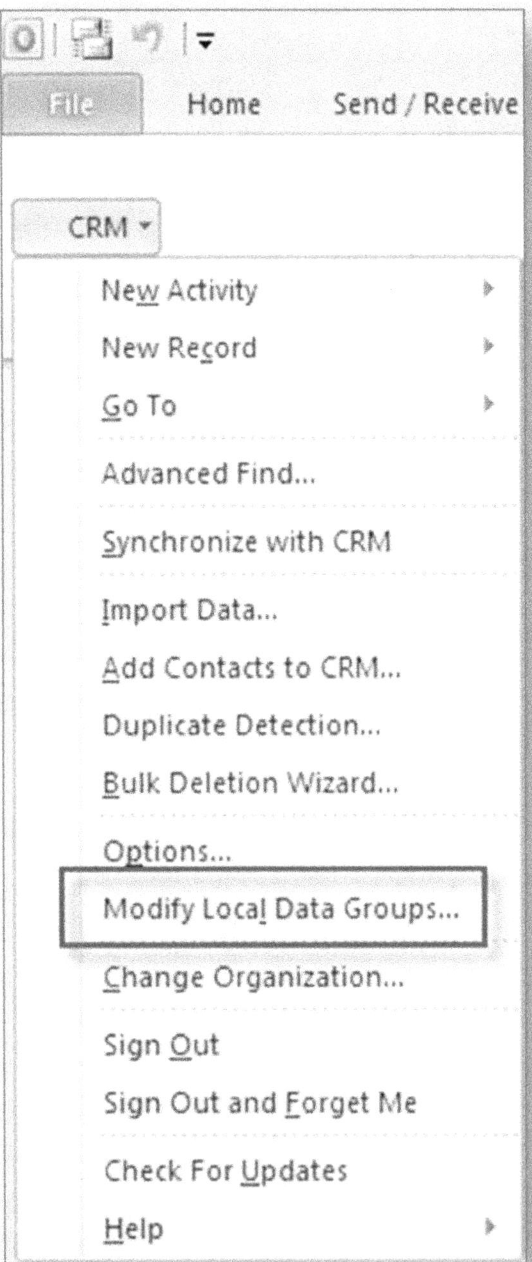

Specifying contacts that should sync down to Outlook

CRM won't sync to your phone, but Outlook does, so any CRM contacts you sync down to Outlook will likely instantly show up on your phone.

Changes made to the contact record on your phone will sync back into Outlook. Then, they'll sync from Outlook back into CRM. All of this happens over-the-air. It's

Step-by-Step Instructions

1. In Outlook, click on the CRM menu. (In Outlook 2010, this is located in the Add-ins tab.)
2. Choose Modify Local Data Groups.
3. Double click My Contacts. The query that appears represents the set of contacts that will sync from CRM down into Outlook.

Tips & Tricks

- For help on building queries, take a look at the Advanced Find lessons in this book.
- Contacts currently in Outlook will not sync up to CRM, unless you click the Track in CRM button.
- Sync happens every 15 minutes. To run a manual sync, click CRM on the menu and choose Synchronize with CRM.

Forcing a synchronization

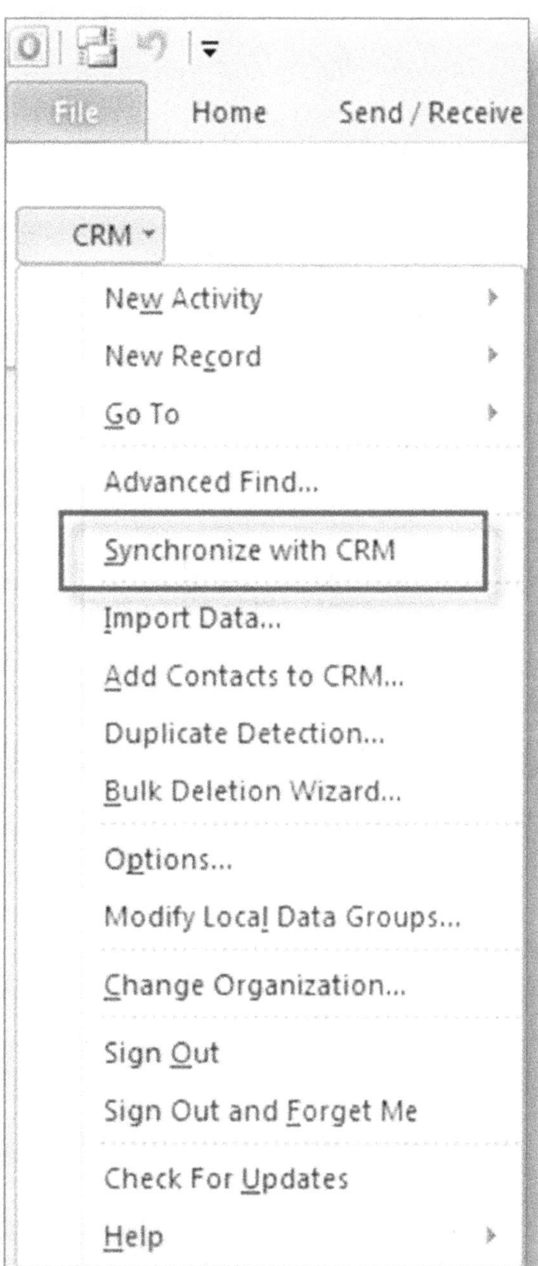

Microsoft Dynamics CRM for Outlook synchronizes contacts, appointments, and tasks automatically every fifteen minutes. But if you are really impatient, you can force synchronization.

You'll only really need to use this if you need to see changes synchronized right away. For example, if you've updated an appointment in CRM and your boss is yelling because he can't see it in Outlook, you'd need to force a sync (or wait for fifteen minutes).

Step-by-Step Instructions

1. In Outlook, locate the CRM menu. In versions 2003/2007, it's on the menu bar. In 2010, it's in the Add-ins tab.
2. Choose the Synchronize with CRM option. This will force all contact, calendar, and e-mail items to sync.

Tips & Tricks

- Your administrator can set the default sync increment for Outlook. 15 minutes is as often as it can happen, though.
- Normally, you won't have to force a sync. Only run these steps when you suspect something isn't synchronizing properly or if you need to see something passed from CRM <-> Outlook instantly.

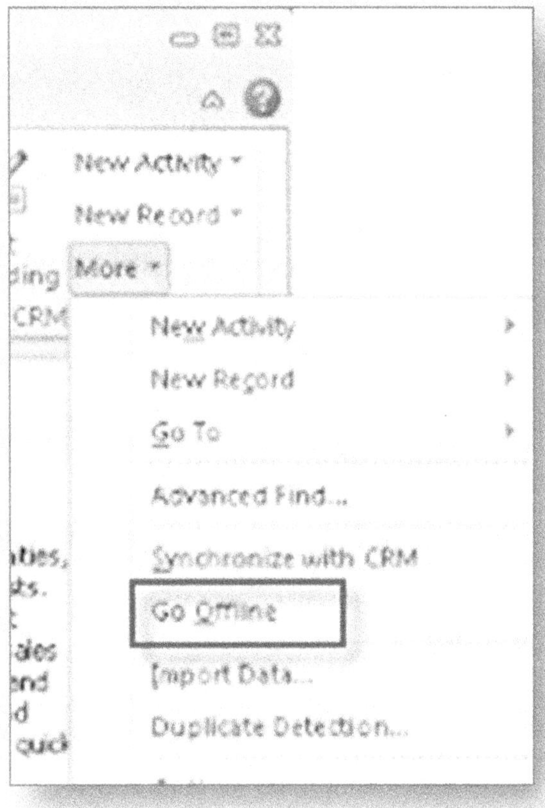

Working offline

Have you decided to spend some time in a cave with no electricity or internet? Well, the offline access feature is just for you! Working offline allows you to disconnect from the Microsoft Dynamics CRM server and still work with records in your database.

When you go offline, Microsoft Dynamics CRM synchronizes selected parts of your CRM database to your local computer. Your changes will synchronize with the online database once you re-enter civilization and connect to the Internet.

Step-by-Step Instructions

1. In Outlook, locate the CRM menu. In versions 2003/2007, it's on the menu bar. In 2010, it's in the Add-ins tab. Choose the Go Offline option.

2. Wait for Microsoft Dynamics CRM to synchronize the data to your computer. When this process is finished you will be working offline.

3. The button you pressed in step one should now say "Go Online." Click it to go back online and synchronize the changes you made to the online database.

Tips & Tricks

- Avoid working offline. It increases the need your need to troubleshoot. It would be better to get a wireless internet card.

Sending contacts from Outlook to CRM

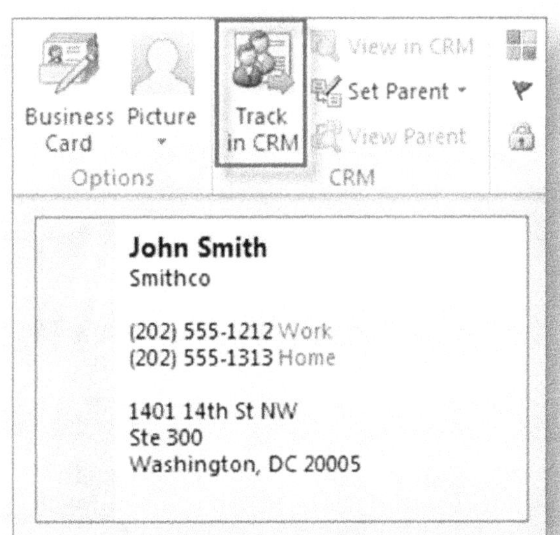

Chances are good that some people in your team have entered their important work contacts into their local Outlook contact lists. Chances are also good that you have personal records in Outlook, too.

With CRM, you can choose which contacts get synchronized up into CRM. (So your dirty little secrets are safe in Outlook and won't go into CRM unless you click the Track in CRM button on them.)

Step-by-Step Instructions

1. In your local Outlook contacts list, locate the contact you'd like to sync with CRM. Highlight it.
2. Click the Track in CRM button on the toolbar. (In Outlook 2010, it's in the Add-ins tab.)

Tips & Tricks

- Once tracked, changes made to a record in either CRM, Outlook, or your phone will sync throughout the system.
- When tracking an Outlook contact in CRM, you also have the option of linking the contact to an existing parent account in CRM.
- Contacts in Public Folders can't be synchronized with CRM. Only contacts in your local Outlook contacts list.

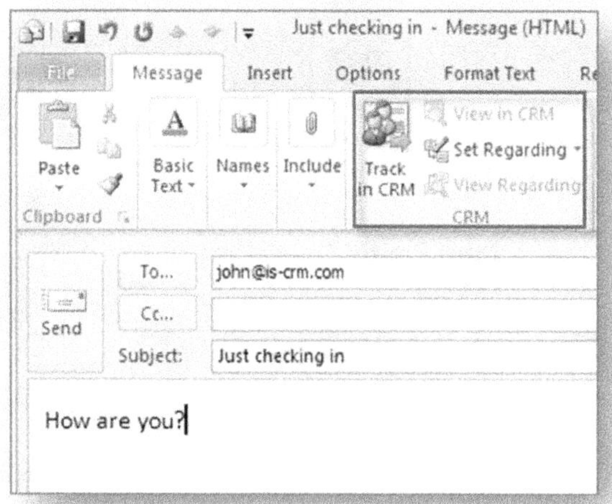

Tracking e-mails in CRM

You just extended a great offer to a customer, but Betty in accounting just sent them a cut-off letter because of late payments.

If everyone in your organization tracked e-mails in CRM, you would have seen Betty's e-mail in the contact's history. Tracking relevant e-mails is a great way to keep everyone in the loop on important correspondence.

Step-by-Step Instructions

1. Create an e-mail message in Outlook.
2. At the top of the screen, click either the Track in CRM or Set Regarding buttons to track back to a CRM record.
3. Send the e-mail message. A copy of the message will show up in the record's history.

Tips & Tricks

- If you click the Track in CRM button, the system will track the e-mail message back to a contact or company using the e-mail address to find the appropriate record.
- Click the Set Regarding button if you want to choose a record for tracking the history.

Tracking appointments and tasks in CRM

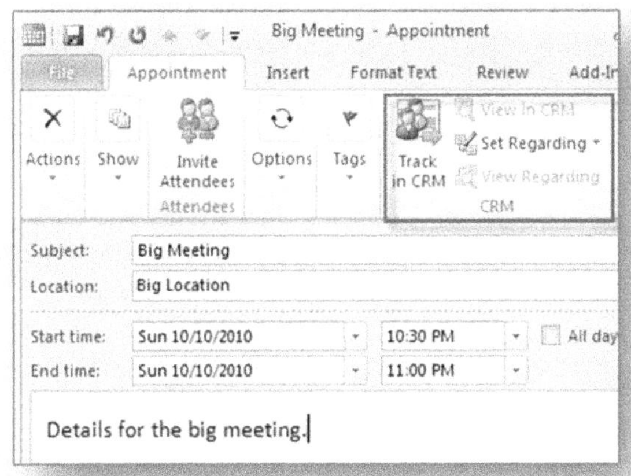

You already manage your tasks and appointments in Outlook, right? Luckily, your Outlook activities can be linked back to CRM records.

Tracking an appointment or task in CRM is similar to tracking a contact or e-mail. Just open an appointment and click the Set Regarding button.

Step-by-Step Instructions

1. Go to your Outlook calendar or task list.
2. Locate an appointment or task and open it.
3. Click either the Track in CRM or Set Regarding buttons. (They're located on the ribbon.)

Tips & Tricks

- In general, you should use the Set Regarding button to relate tasks and appointments back to CRM records.
- If you are sending a meeting request, and if the recipient's email address matches up with a record in CRM, then you can just click the Track in CRM button.

CHAPTER

3

Getting your records into the system

Creating a new record ◆ Deleting or deactivating a record ◆ Importing records ◆ Importing records ◆ Creating relationships ◆ Assigning records to other users ◆ Sharing records with other users ◆ Copying/ sending shortcuts to records ◆ Bulk deleting records

Creating a new record

You can't have a database without data, so you will need to learn how to create records before using Microsoft Dynamics CRM.

Accounts, contacts, leads, opportunities, and activities are all examples of records. They are the meat and potatoes of your database, and creating them is simple.

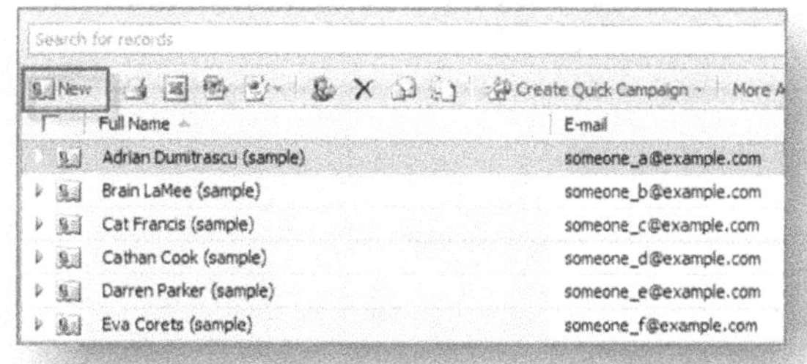

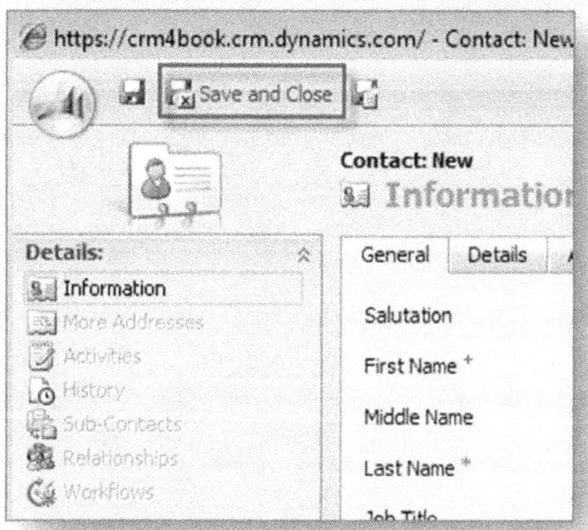

Step-by-Step Instructions

1. Click Sales in the Navigation Pane, and then click Contacts.
2. Click the New button on the Actions Toolbar.
3. Enter information about the record. Click Save and Close.

Tips & Tricks

➢ Instead of creating records from scratch, you can import from an existing data source, like an Excel spreadsheet. Just click Tools | Import on the menu.

Deleting or deactivating a record

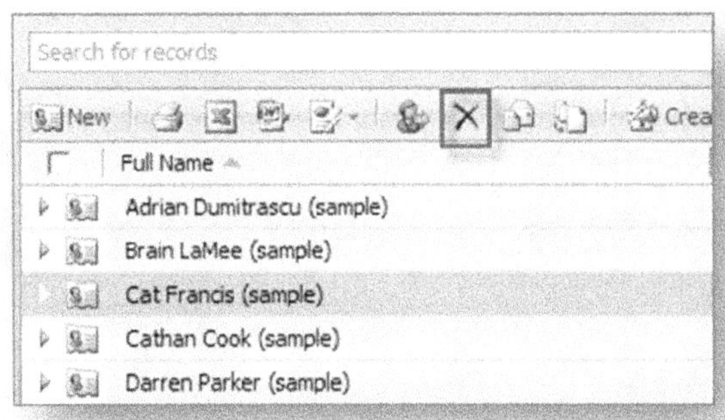

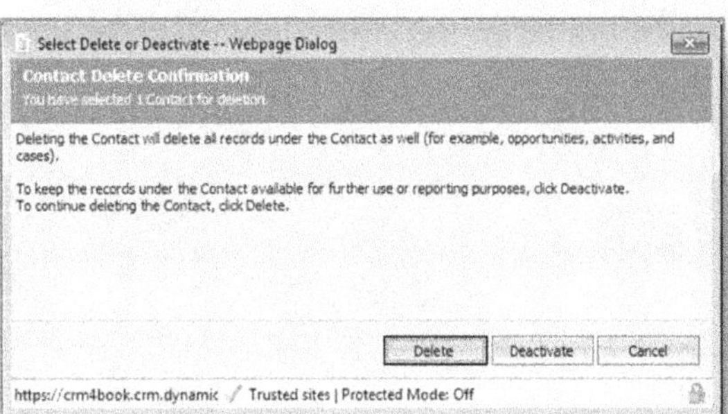

Have you ever gotten into an argument with one of your contacts and thought, "Wow, I'd like to wipe you from my database?" Microsoft Dynamics CRM allows you to do this by either deleting or deactivating a record.

Deleted records can't be retrieved, so be careful before you delete a record. A deactivated record stays in the database with an inactive status, but won't appear in your active records.

Step-by-Step Instructions

1. Click Sales in the Navigation Pane, and then click Contacts.
2. Highlight the contact that you want to delete.
3. On the Actions toolbar, click the delete icon. (It looks like an X.)
4. Click Yes to confirm the deletion.

Tips & Tricks

- This process walks you through the steps required to delete a contact, but these steps will work on just about any entity in the system.
- If you don't see an option to delete, you might not have access to delete records.

Importing records

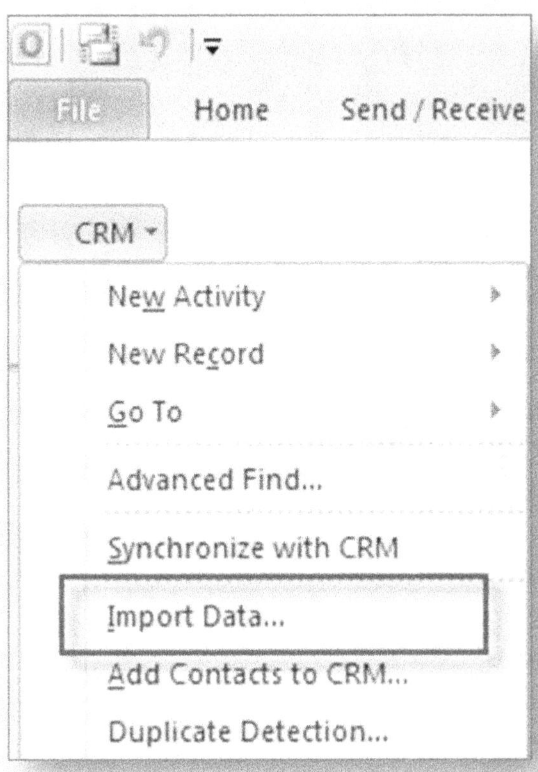

Entering in records manually is a hassle. If your data already exists in electronic format, you'll need to learn to import records.

You might, for instance, have a spreadsheet of records that you want in CRM. By importing this file, you can spend less time entering data and more time selling or playing Solitaire.

Step-by-Step Instructions

1. On the menu, click Tools and then Import.
2. Click Browse and look for your file. Click Next.
3. Select the type of record and data map. Click next
4. Select a record owner and click next.
5. Give the import a name and click Import.

Data file name:
Browse...
Supported file types: XML Spreadsheet 2003 (.xml), .csv, .txt, and .zip

Tips & Tricks

- You can import XML, CSV, TXT, and other basic data files into CRM. If your data is currently in another format, like ACT! or Goldmine, then you may consider having a consultant run your import to maintain notes, histories, activities, opportunities, etc.

Creating relationships

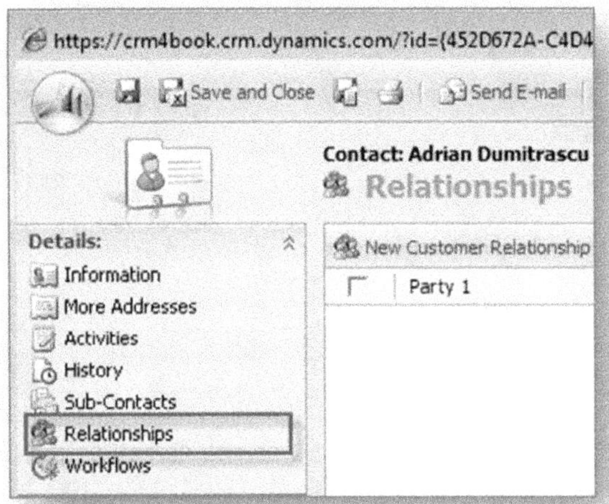

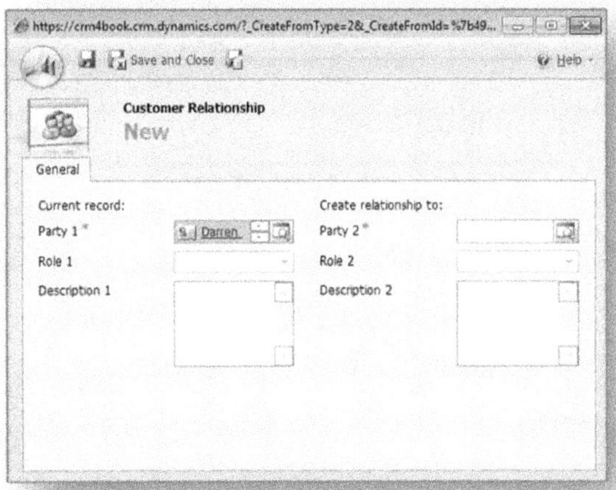

Relationships can be hard to manage. Fortunately, Microsoft Dynamics CRM can help you keep track of a complicated relationship between different entities in your database.

In Microsoft Dynamics CRM you can create relationship roles, which can then be applied to records in the database. Examples of relationship roles could be: lawyer, family member, boss, subordinate, etc.

Step-by-Step Instructions

1. Open an account or contact record.
2. On the left, click the Relationships option. All of the existing relationships for this record will appear.
3. Click the New button to create a new relationship between this record an another account or contact.

Tips & Tricks

- Before setting a relationship, you'll need to have roles set up in the system. Go to Settings | Business Management | Relationship Roles.

Assigning records to other users

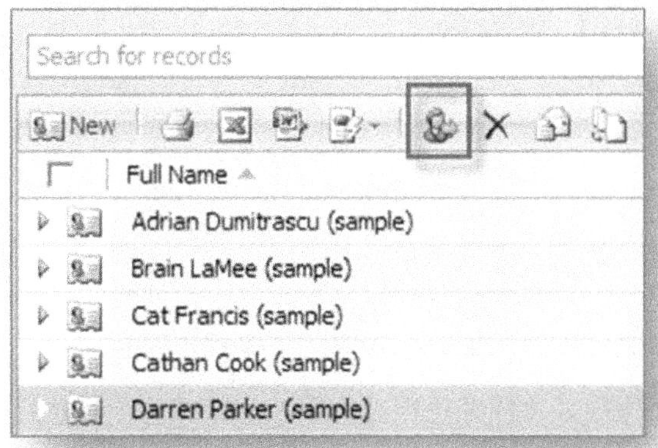

Do you have an annoying customer that you want to unload onto the guy in the cubicle next to yours? Fortunately, Microsoft Dynamics CRM lets you re-assign records to other users.

Whenever you create a new record, that record is assigned to you. You can re-assign ownership of the record as long as you have the user rights to do so.

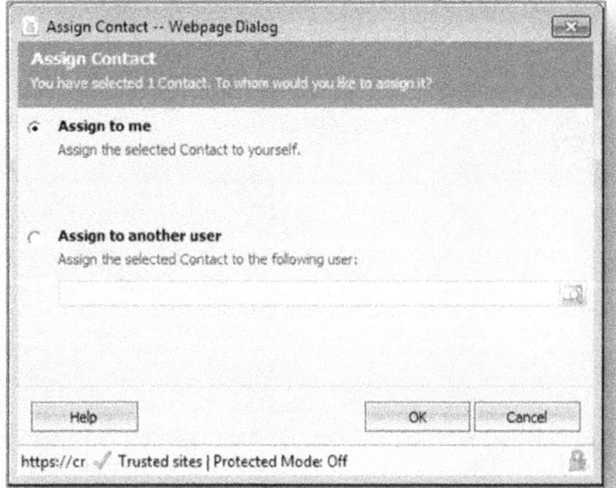

Step-by-Step Instructions

1. Click Sales, then Accounts on the Navigation Pane.
2. Highlight the record you want assign.
3. Click the Assign button on the toolbar. (It looks like a person with an arrow.)
4. Choose a user to whom you'd like to assign the record, or assign it to yourself.

Tips & Tricks

➢ You may not have access to assign records in your system, so if you get an error, contact your system administrator.

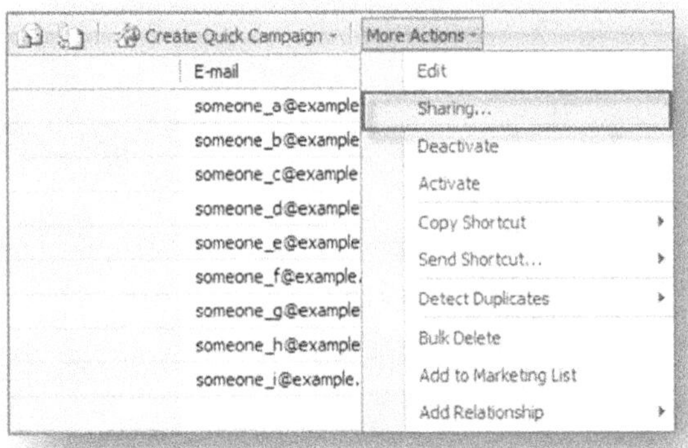

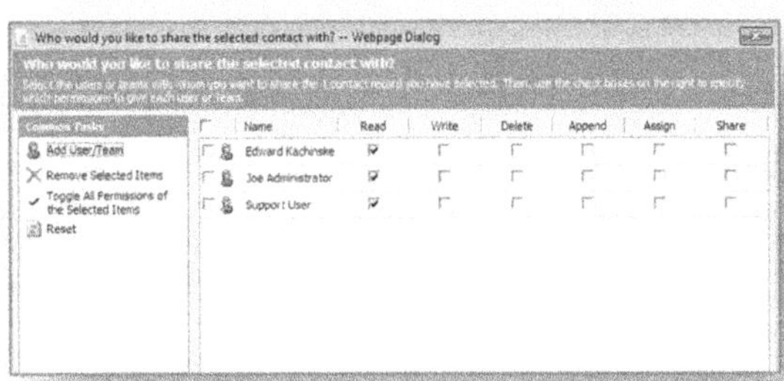

Sharing records with other users

Sharing is an important virtue - one that we all learned when we were young. Well, it's also a feature built into Microsoft Dynamics CRM.

Your database might be set up so that only a record owner can see his or her own records. A record owner then has the option to share his or her record with another user or group of users.

Step-by-Step Instructions

1. Click Sales, then Accounts on the Navigation Pane.
2. Highlight the account you want to share.
3. Under More Actions, click Sharing.
4. Click Add User/Team and find the user or team you'd like to share the record with.

Tips & Tricks

➢ These steps are written for accounts, but you can share any record in the system by clicking More Actions | Sharing.

Copying / sending shortcuts to records

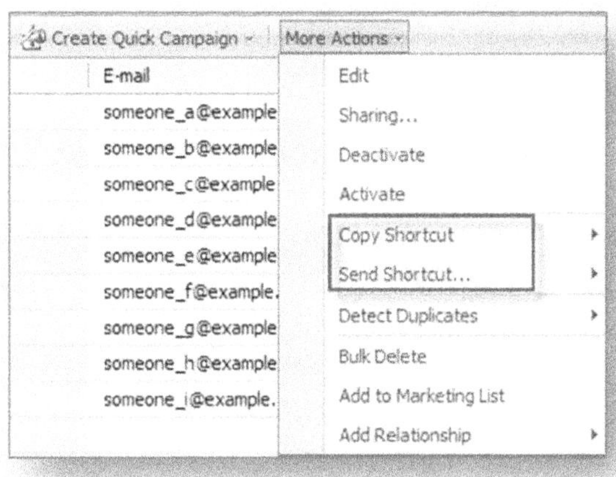

So the guy in the cube next to you didn't go to CRM training. And he asked you *again* to look up someone's phone number.

Instead of just giving him the number, you could give him a shortcut to the record in CRM, and as long as he's a valid CRM user, he could click that link to bring up the record directly in CRM.

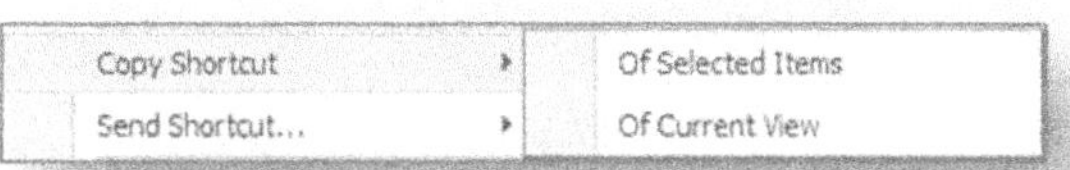

Step-by-Step Instructions

1. Go to any record in CRM. This could be a contact, account, opportunity, or other type of record.
2. On the Actions drop-down, choose to either copy or send a shortcut for the current record.
3. The shortcut will either open in an Outlook e-mail message, or it will be copied to the clipboard.

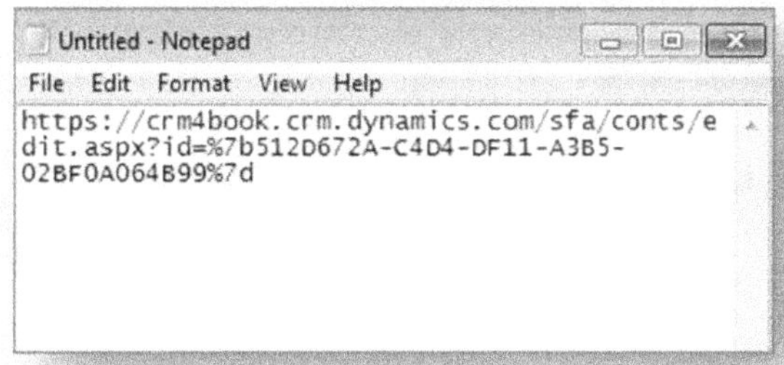

Tips & Tricks

- Non-CRM users won't be able to view record shortcuts. Only users with a valid CRM login will be able to see your CRM records.
- If you want to grant access to outside users, consider creating a customer portal with the CRM Online Portal Accelerator. (It's available on Codeplex.com.)

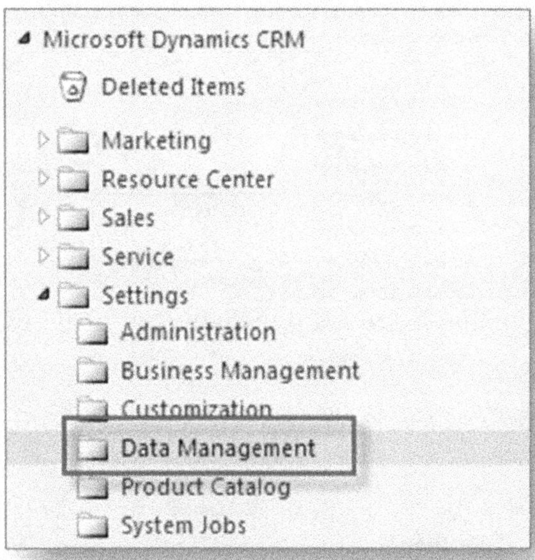

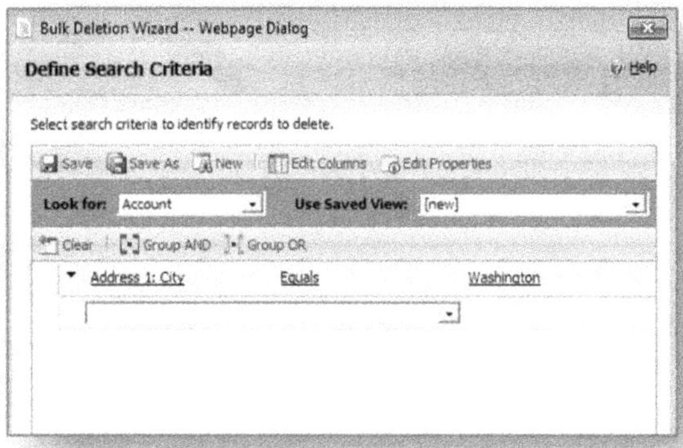

Bulk deleting records

You just got laid off, and you don't have anything to do until the end of the day. So why not delete your former company's entire database? It's easy to do with a bulk delete. Best of all, there is no way to undo a bulk delete.

In all seriousness, this is a feature that should likely be turned off for most users, especially the ones you've laid off.

Step-by-Step Instructions

1. On the navigation bar, click Settings and then Data Management.

2. Click Bulk Record Deletion.

3. Click the New button to create a new bulk deletion job.

4. Follow the instructions on the wizard to create a query of records to delete. Any records matching careful.)

Tips & Tricks

- Make sure you have a backup of any records before you bulk delete them.

- Be careful of this feature.

CHAPTER

4

Organizing your hectic life with activities in CRM Online

Using the Activities view in CRM ◆ Viewing your calendar in CRM ◆ Creating follow-up activities from a record ◆ Viewing pending activities and past history associated with a record

Using the Activities view in CRM

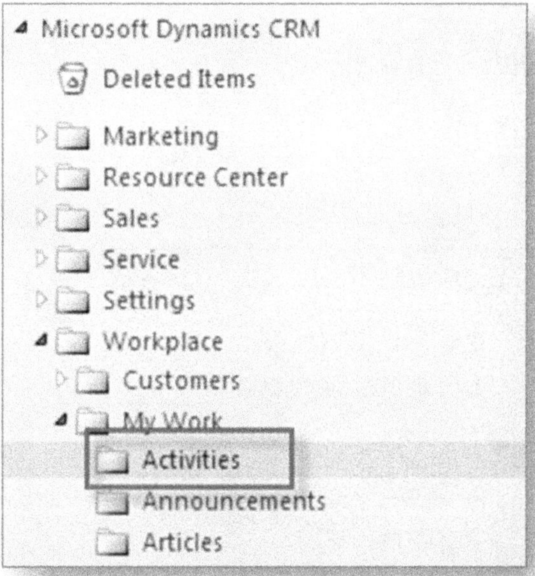

Microsoft Dynamics CRM is much more than a fancy rolodex that keeps track of your contacts. It will also help you manage activities, such as phone calls, tasks, e-mails, letters, and appointments.

The activities view in Microsoft Dynamics CRM lets you work with activities that have been tracked in the CRM system.

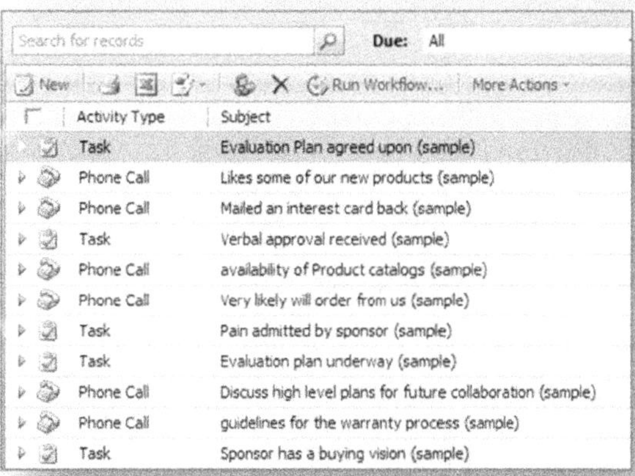

Step-by-Step Instructions

1. On the Navigation pane, click the Workplace option and choose Activities.
2. Use the filter at the top of the screen to set the activities you'd like to see.
3. Any changes made to activities in this view will sync to Outlook automatically.

Tips & Tricks

- Think of this Activities view as a great way to create simple activity reports. You could, for example, bring up a list of all high priority tasks finished this week, and then you could export this list to Excel for pivot table reporting.

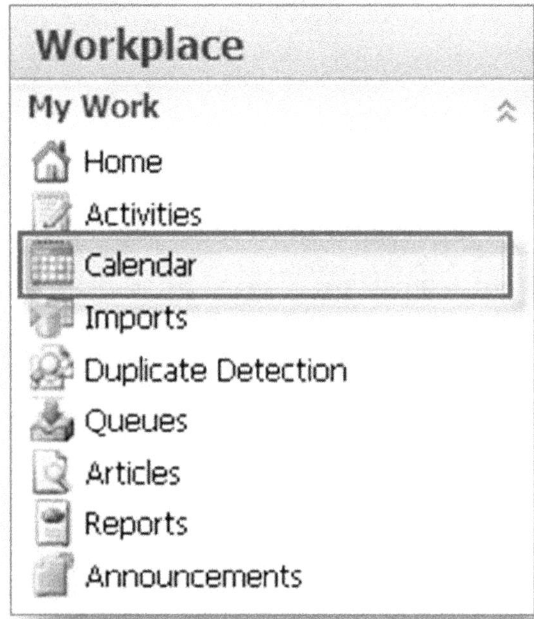

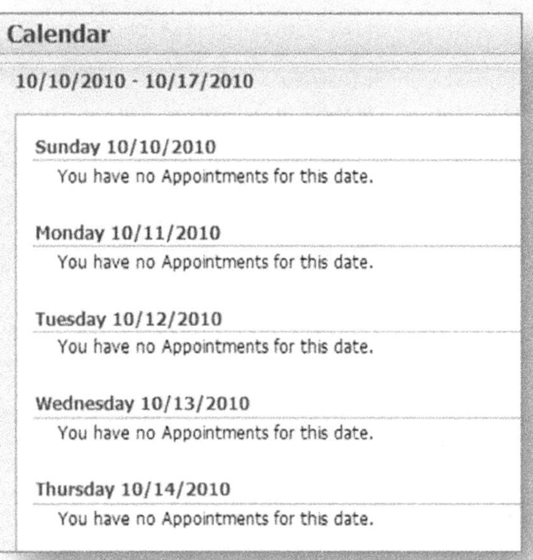

Viewing your calendar in CRM

Calendars make your life a whole lot easier, even if they do give you a lot of work to do. Using the calendar in Microsoft Dynamics CRM is simple and can help you visualize your schedule.

The calendar in CRM can be viewed by day, week, or month. Outlook activities show up in your CRM calendar if you track them in CRM.

Having said that, the Outlook calendar will give you a better user experience, so you'd likely be better off managing your calendar directly within Outlook.

Step-by-Step Instructions

1. On the Navigation Pane, click the Workplace option and choose Calendar.
2. Your calendar will appear. From here, you can see your schedule, add new activities, and edit any activities that have been tracked to CRM.

Tips & Tricks

- This calendar view will *only* show activities that have been tracked in CRM. If you have any Outlook activities that aren't linked to CRM records, then you should ignore this view and work directly within Outlook.

Creating follow-up activities from a record

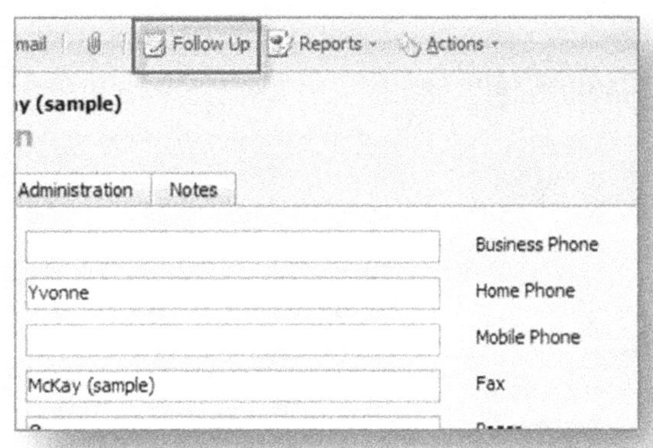

How would your customers feel if you never called them back? You may want to spare them any hard feelings by creating a follow-up activity. Follow-up activities can be created for any type of record, and it's really simple -- you will never even have to leave the form.

Any activity created using this method will be automatically associated with its record, and the activity will show up in your Outlook calendar.

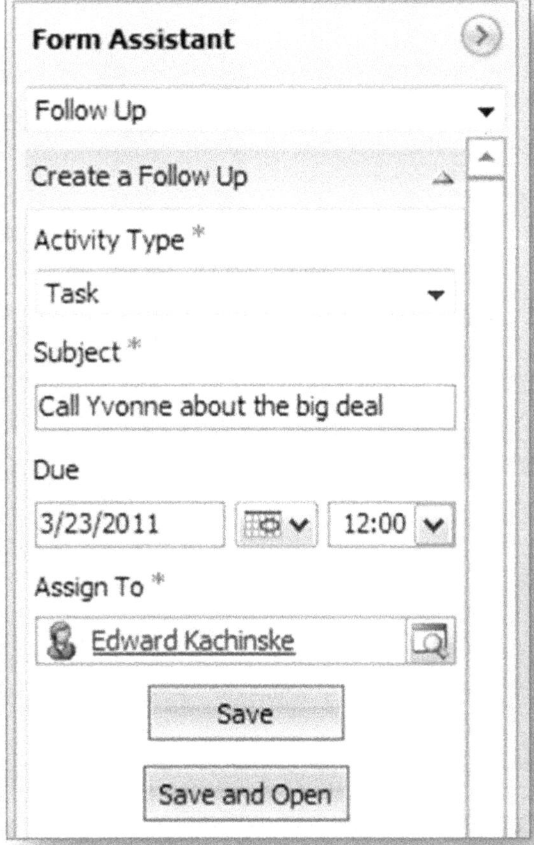

Step-by-Step Instructions

1. Open a record. For example, you might open a company or contact record.
2. On the toolbar click the Follow Up button.
3. A form assistant will appear on the right of the record. Enter details for your follow-up task or appointment and click Save.

Tips & Tricks

- If you often create follow-up tasks for records, consider automating the process with a workflow. With the workflow feature, you can turn this whole process into a single click on the toolbar.

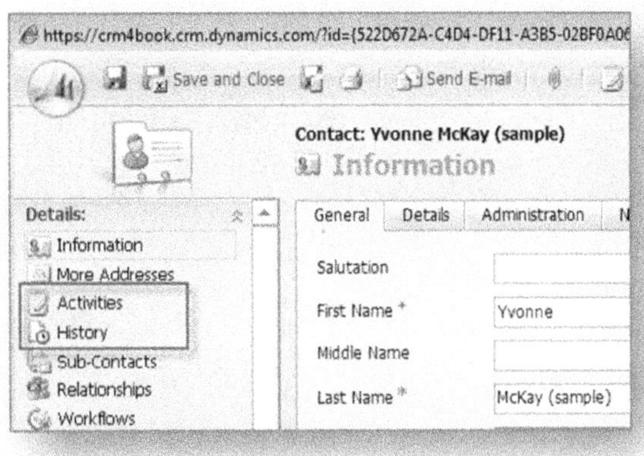

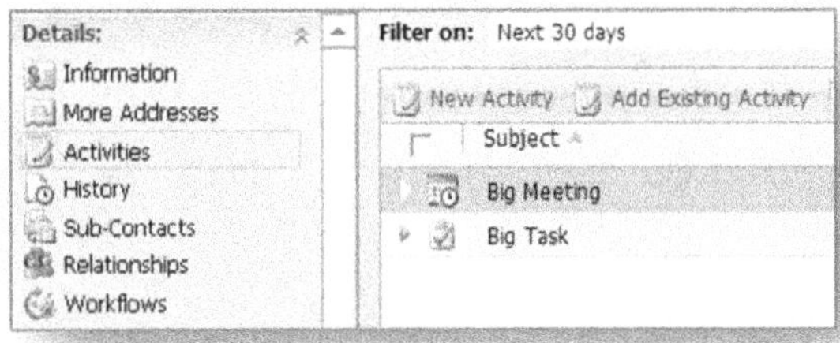

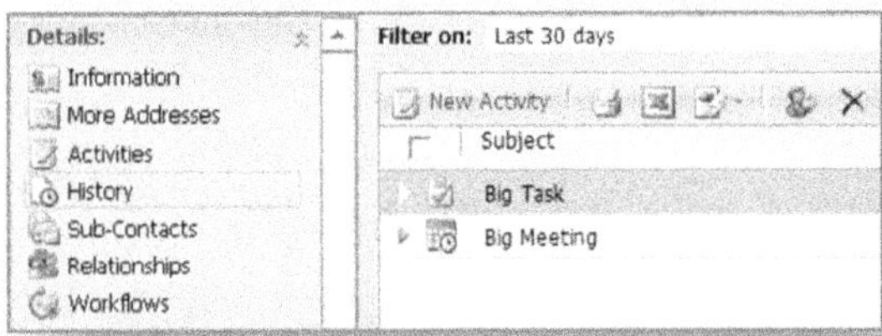

Viewing pending activities and past history associated with a record

You may remember what you've done with a contact or company in your database, but you may not be aware of the tasks and e-mails that others have done with a record.

In the Activities and History tabs within CRM, you can get a full picture of all activities, e-mails, and tasks that have been entered by anyone in your organization.

Step-by-Step Instructions

1. Open a record. For example, you might open a company or contact record.

2. On the left, click the Activities option. A list of pending activities scheduled with the record will appear.

3. Now, click the History option. This will show a list of e-mails sent, as well as past appointments and tasks that have been completed.

Tips & Tricks

- Using an iframe, you can add activities and history to the main screen on your record form.

Dealing with duplicates and dealing with duplicates.

Scanning for duplicates ◆ Merging duplicates ◆ Enabling duplicate detection in the system ◆ Modifying duplicate detection rules

Scanning for duplicates

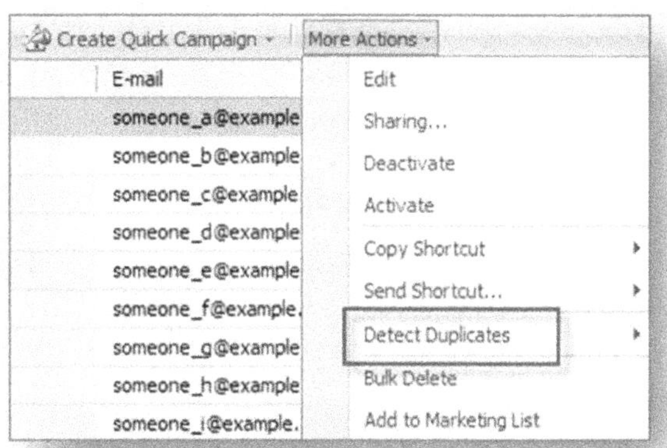

Believe it or not, mistakes can be made during data-entry. And duplicates are definitely annoying. And duplicates are definitely annoying.

Duplicate records in your database can cause you a lot of trouble, especially if they go unnoticed. Fortunately, Microsoft Dynamics CRM can help you automatically find duplicate records and deal with them so that you can maintain a clean database.

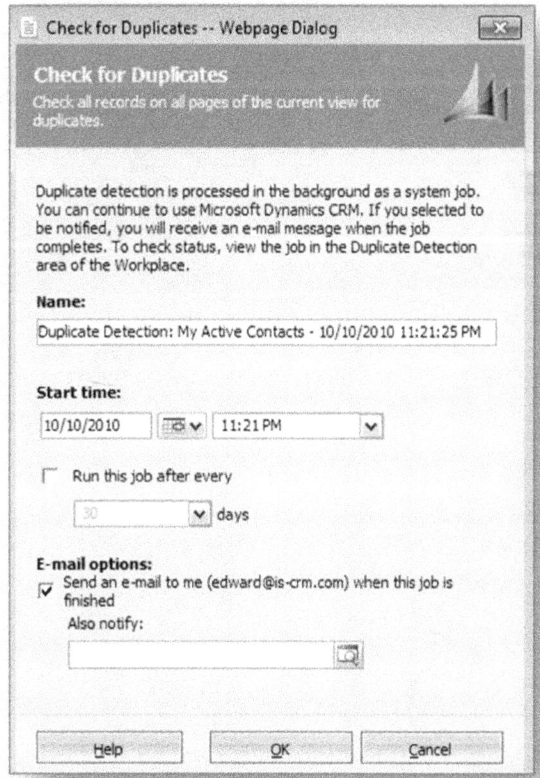

Step-by-Step Instructions

1. Click on a list of records on the Navigation Pane, such as Accounts.
2. Click the More Actions drop-down on the toolbar. Click Detect Duplicates.
3. Give the duplicate detection job a name, start time, and frequency. Click OK.

Tips & Tricks

➢ When creating a duplicate detection job, you have the option to narrow the job to a subset of the database. Setting a query in the duplicate detection wizard will narrow down the range of records searched. For example, you might only want to find duplicates that you own.

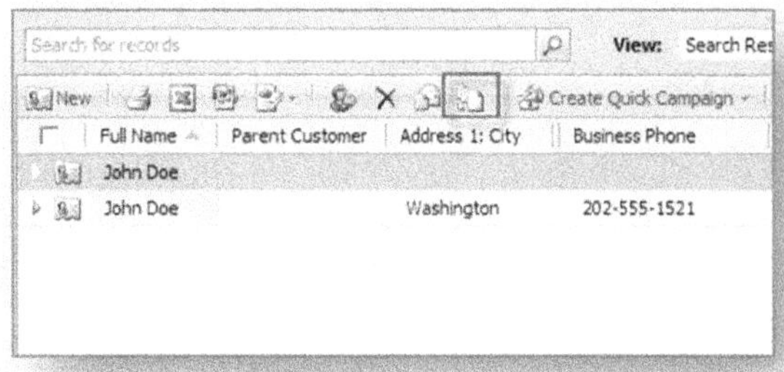

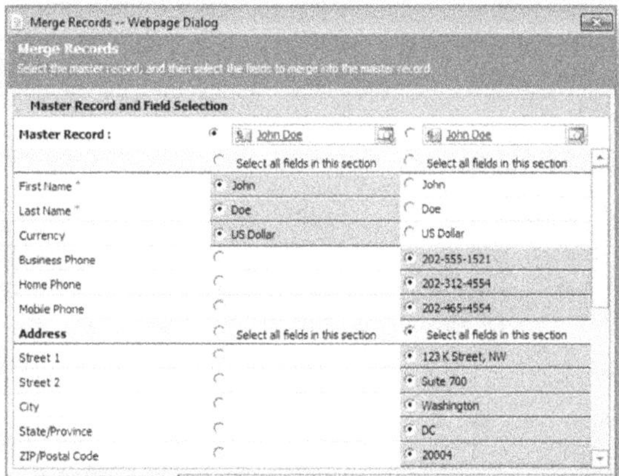

Merging duplicates

Have you found a duplicate record in your system? Rather than simply trashing one of the found records, you should use the merging feature in Microsoft Dynamics CRM.

This feature gives you complete control over duplicate merging and is really easy to use. Duplicate records are lined up side by side so that you can decide which fields you want to keep in the merged record.

Step-by-Step Instructions

1. Find the two duplicate records. Hold Ctrl and click on each record. They should both be highlighted.
2. Click Merge on the Actions Toolbar.
3. Highlight a master record. This should be the record that is more complete.
4. Highlight all of the field values that should be kept in the merged record.

Tips & Tricks

- Once you merge records, notes/histories/opportunities/etc from both records are combined.
-
- There is a checkbox at the bottom of the merge screen. It allows you to select all fields with data. It's a good idea to always click this box when merging duplicates.

Enabling duplicate detection in the system

Why go through the trouble of dealing with duplicates when you can proactively keep them out of the database.

Configure Microsoft Dynamics CRM to automatically detect duplicates in the system, and then if you enter a record that is already in CRM, the system will warn you.

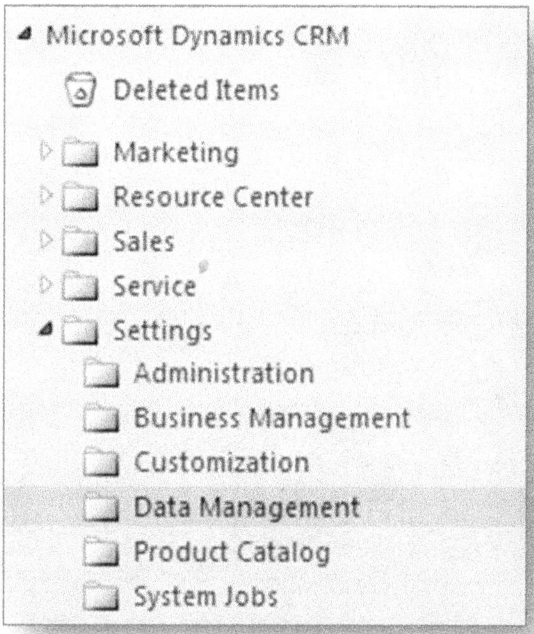

Step-by-Step Instructions

1. On the Navigation Pane, click Settings and then Data Management.
2. Click Duplicate Detection Settings.
3. Choose to either enable or disable duplicate detection in the system.

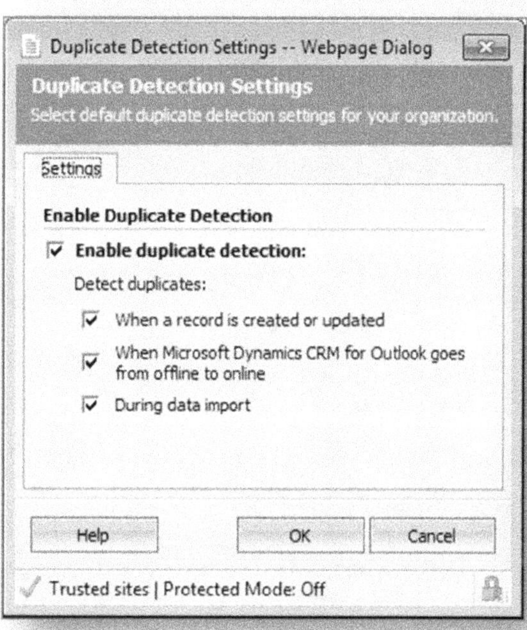

Tips & Tricks

- Duplicate detection occurs when importing and also when adding new records to CRM.
- If you enable duplicate detection, make sure that your duplicate detection rules are fine tuned. (Check out the next page for info on the rules.)

Modifying duplicate detection rules

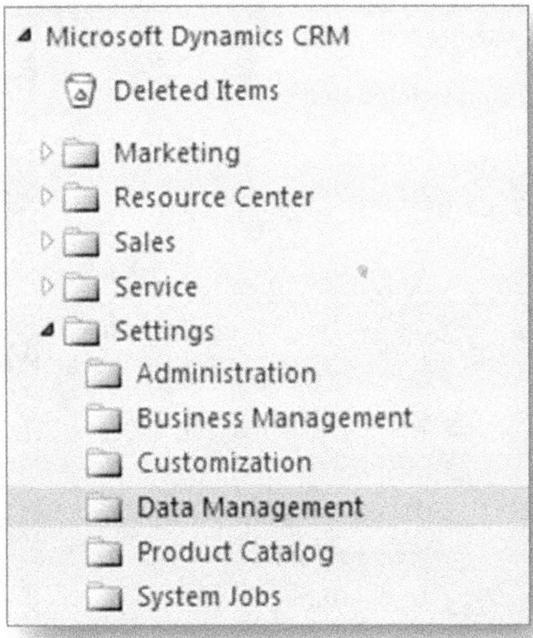

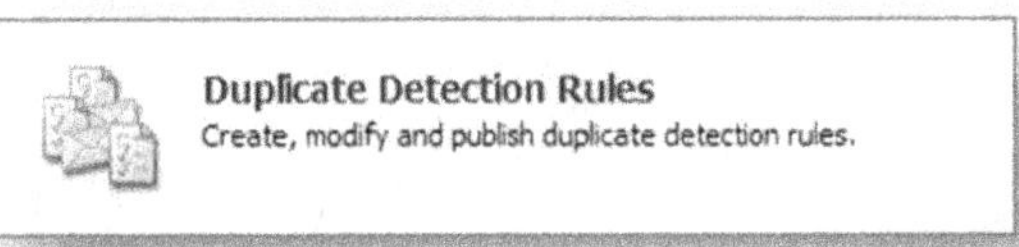

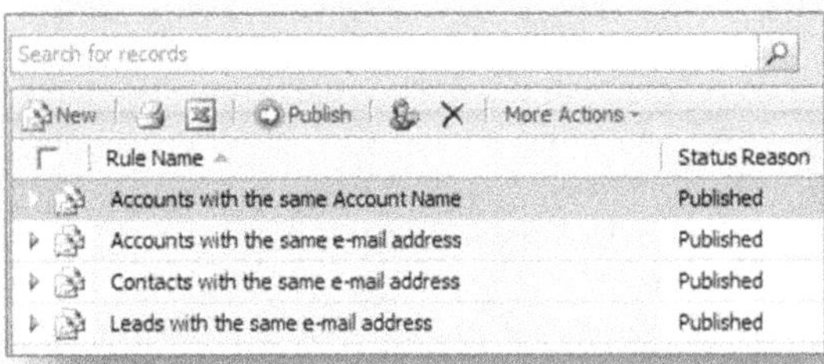

Duplicate detection has a built in set of rules, and while these might work well out of the box, they might not be right for you.

Computers can do great things, but they can't read your mind, and sometimes Microsoft Dynamics CRM will identify records as duplicates even though you want to keep them separate.

Step-by-Step Instructions

1. On the Navigation Pane, click Settings and then Data Management.
2. Click Duplicate Detection Rules.
3. Click the New button to create a new duplicate detection rule.

Tips & Tricks

- The out-of-the-box rules might also not be strong enough. By default, CRM only identifies duplicate contacts as contacts with the same e-mail address.
- Adding additional rules (like a rule that finds contacts with the same last name and zip code) might yield more results in a duplicate detection job.

CHAPTER

6

Where the heck is that record?

Finding records with the quick find feature ◆ Changing the fields that are searched during a Quick Find ◆ Running an Advanced Find ◆ Changing the columns that appear in Advanced Find results ◆ Saving an Advanced Find as a personal view ◆ Sharing your personal views with other users and teams ◆ Searching across entities

Finding records with the Quick Find feature

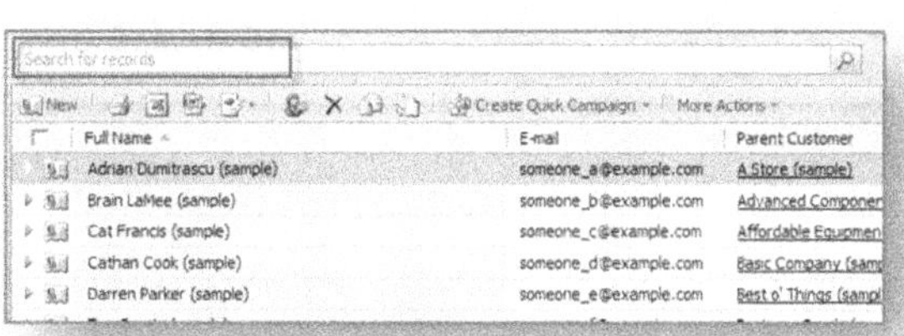

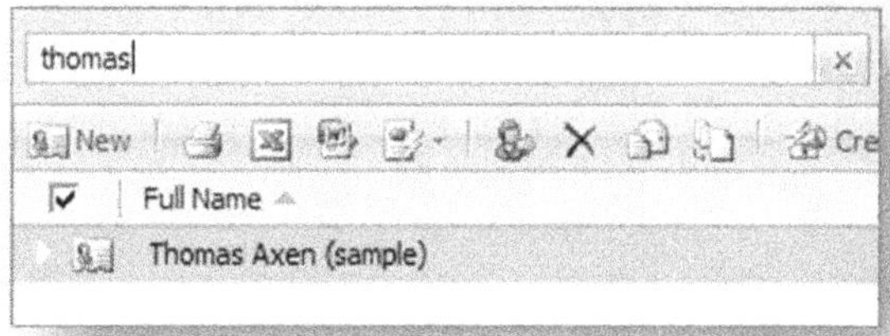

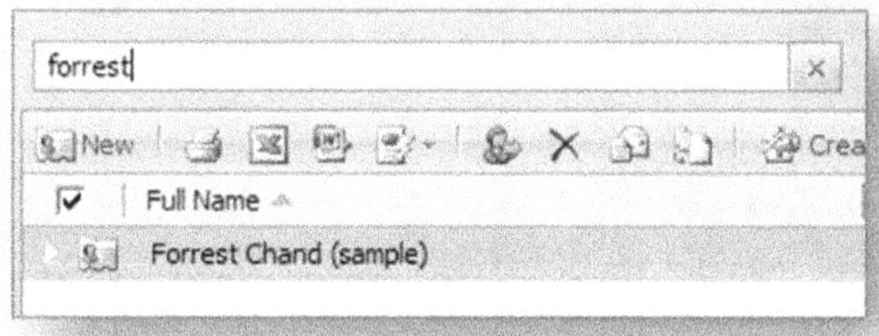

If you need to find a record quickly and easily, then Quick Find is your friend. Sure, it may not be as clever as its big brother (the Advanced Find feature), but it's fast and simple so you'll be using it a lot.

If you need to find a contact by first/last name, you should use a Quick Find.

Step-by-Step Instructions

1. Click on a record type in the Navigation Pane. For example, you could click on Contacts.

2. You'll see a search field at the top of the record list.

3. Enter your search term into the field. Click the magnifying glass button or press Enter to execute the search.

Tips & Tricks

- The Quick Find feature searches on specific fields, but not all fields. To change the fields that are searched, follow the instructions on the next page.

- Use an asterisk (*) as a wild card. This is especially useful when searching for companies that begin with the word *The*.

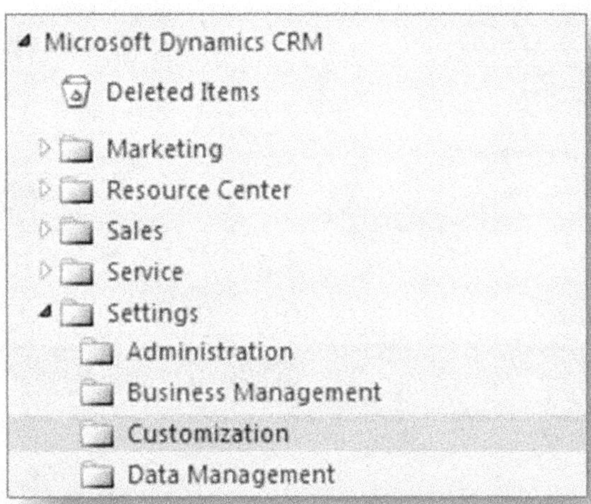

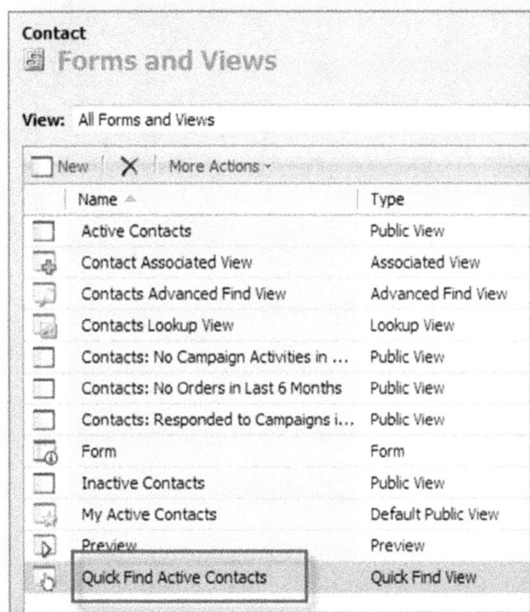

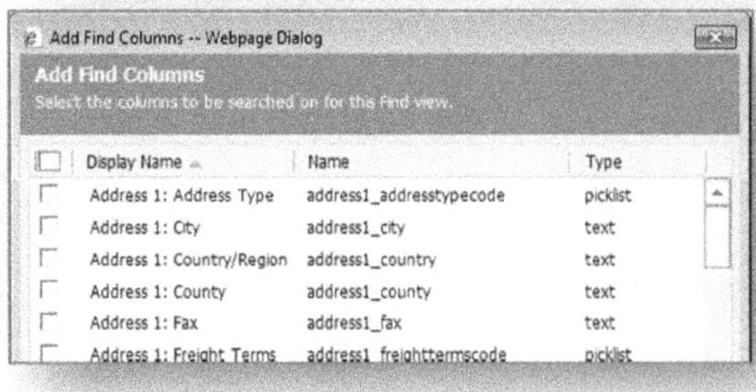

Changing the fields that are searched during a Quick Find

Quick Find is quick because it only searches certain fields. In each record type, Microsoft sets the fields that are searched during a Quick Find. If these default fields work for you, great!

If you aren't satisfied with your Quick Finds results, though, you can change the fields that are searched during a Quick Find.

Step-by-Step Instructions

1. Click Settings on the Navigation Pane, and then click Customization.
2. Click Customize Entities and double click an entity.
3. On the left, click Forms and Views, then double-click the Quick Find View.
4. Click Add Find Columns on the right. Check off any fields that you want to be searched and click OK.
5. Click Save and Close. Remember to publish your customizations.

Tips & Tricks

- Once you have added Quick Find views, click the Publish button to immediately enforce the changes.

Running an Advanced Find

If you want to view a really specific data set, then you'll want to use Advanced Find. Running an Advanced Find is a bit more complicated than running a Quick Find, but it allows you more control over the search process. Advanced Find, for example, lets you search multiple fields at once.

An Advanced Find can also be saved as a view, so if you run a search often, this is likely your fastest option.

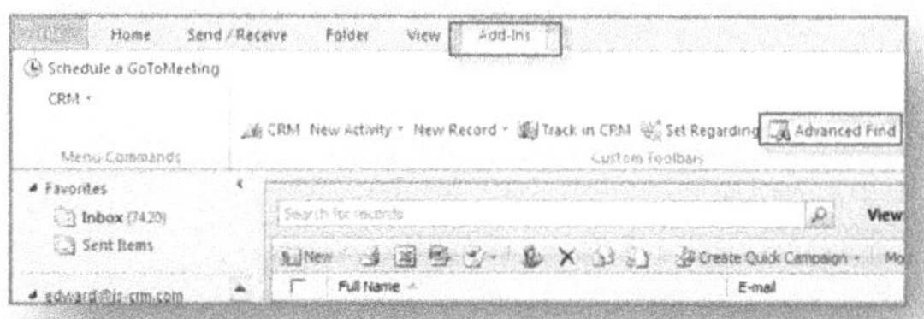

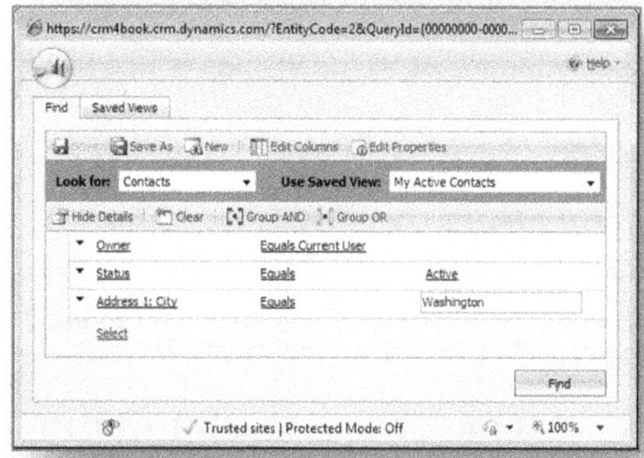

Step-by-Step Instructions

1. Click Advanced Find button on the toolbar.
2. Choose an entity type from the drop-down.
3. Configure your query. (If in doubt, start by hovering your mouse over the <u>Select</u> text.
4. Click Find.

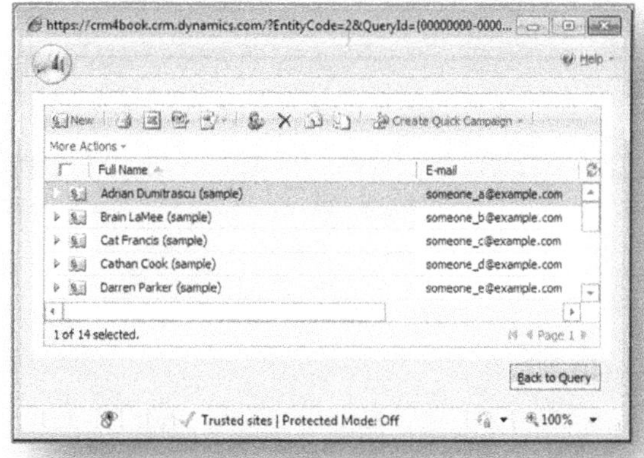

Tips & Tricks

- To customize the **default** set of columns that appear when you click the Find button, go to Settings | Customization | Customize Entities. Double-click your record type and in the Forms & Views area, customize the Advanced Find view.

Changing the columns that appear in Advanced Find results

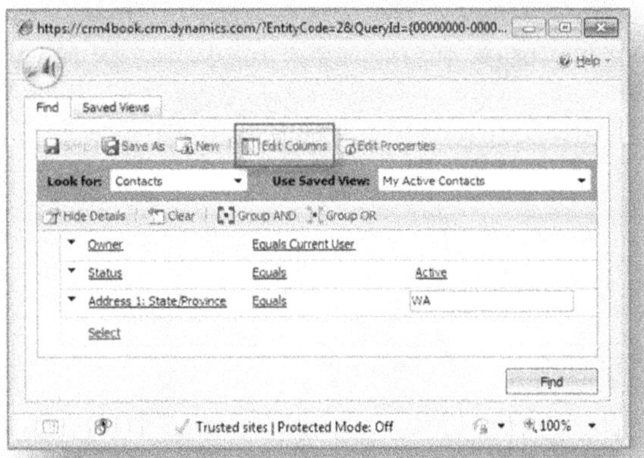

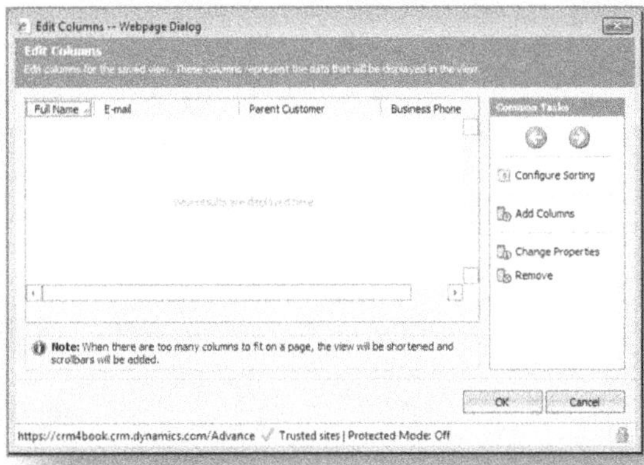

Have you run an Advanced Find but don't exactly like what you see? Then change the columns that appear in your Advanced Find results.

This can be especially useful if you want to perform a mail merge from an Advanced Find, as you can specify that you'd like to add fields like the address fields. Columns added will also appear in your view if you decide to save the Advanced Find as a view.

Step-by-Step Instructions

1. Click Advanced Find on the toolbar.
2. Configure your query.
3. Click Edit Columns. You can then add and remove columns.
4. Click OK and run the Advanced Find.

Tips & Tricks

- After clicking Edit Columns, use the green arrow buttons to move the order of columns.
- Double-click a column header to set its default width.

Saving an Advanced Find as a personal view

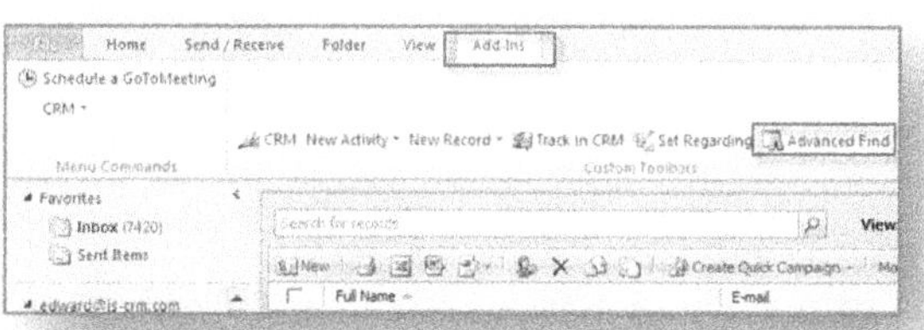

Do you ever find yourself running the same search over and over again? In Microsoft Dynamics CRM, you can save yourself from this hassle by saving your Advanced Find as a personal view.

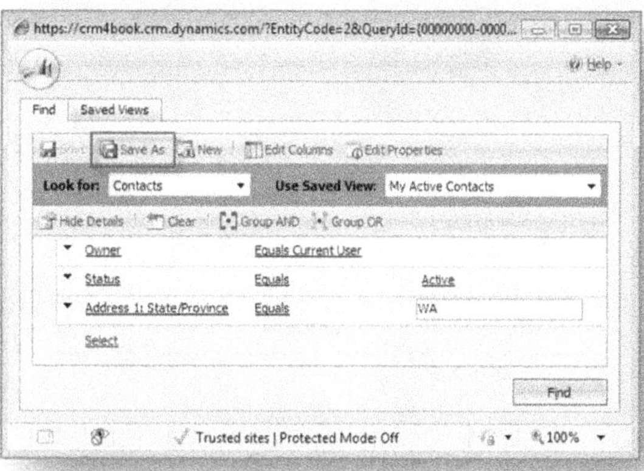

Search results displayed in a saved view will be updated as your database changes. For example, if you save an Advanced Find that shows all current opportunities, the view will always give you the complete list of current opportunities. If you close an opportunity, it is removed from the view automatically.

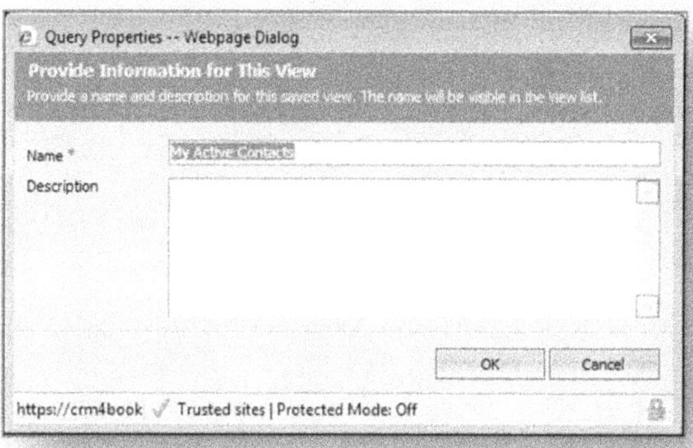

Step-by-Step Instructions

1. Click the Advanced Find button on the toolbar.
2. Set up your query.
3. Click Save As on the Actions Toolbar.
4. Give your view a name.
5. Exit the Advanced Find.
6. Refresh. The Advanced Find should now show up in your list of views.

Tips & Tricks

- You can share the view with others. See the next page...

Sharing your personal views with other users and teams

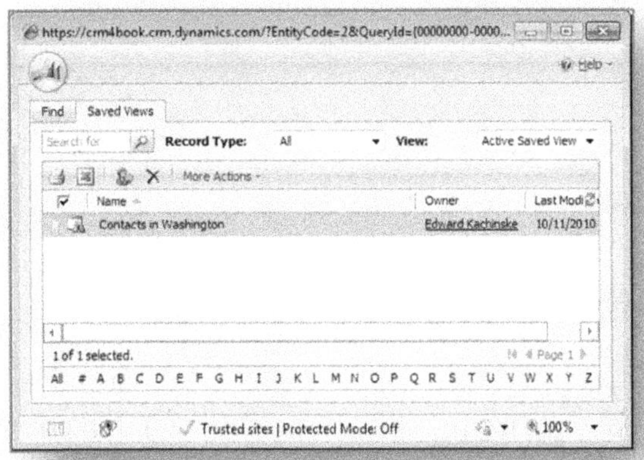

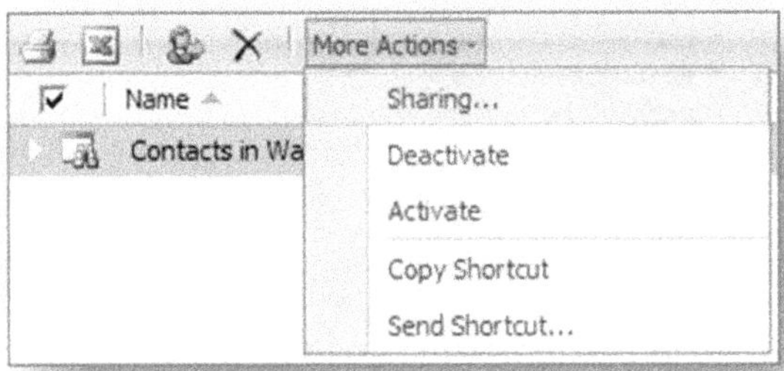

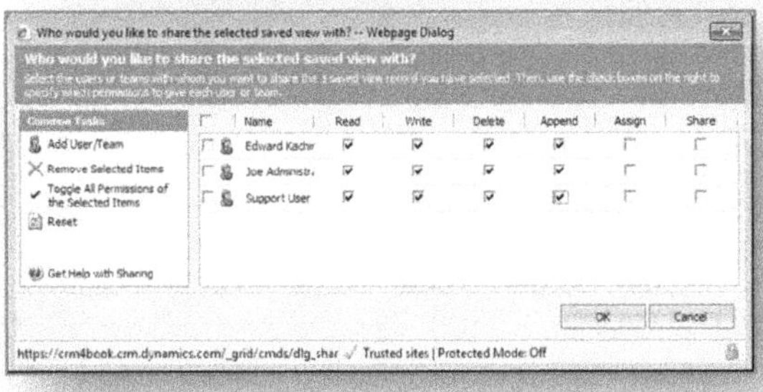

Have you come up with a really useful Advanced Find that you've saved as a personal view? Does someone else in your office want to use it?

Well, quit bogarting that view, dude! Share it! (And if you don't know what bogarting is, ask your kids or look it up on Bing.)

Step-by-Step Instructions

1. Click the Advanced Find Button on the toolbar, and configure your query and column settings. Save the view.

2. Click the Saved Views Tab.

2. Highlight the saved view. Click More Actions on the toolbar, then Sharing.

3. Add or remove users and click OK.

Tips & Tricks

- When sharing a view with others, you may want to restrict what they can do with the view. For example, sharing a view without giving someone Write access will ensure that they don't mess up the view.
- If you need to share with multiple users, share it with a team.

Searching across entities

Most of the Advanced Find examples you'll run across will only involve one entity. So, you'll search for all contacts in Washington, DC. All opportunities greater than $50,000. And so on.

But let's say you want to search for all opportunities greater than $50K that are associated with an account in DC. That search requires searching across entities.

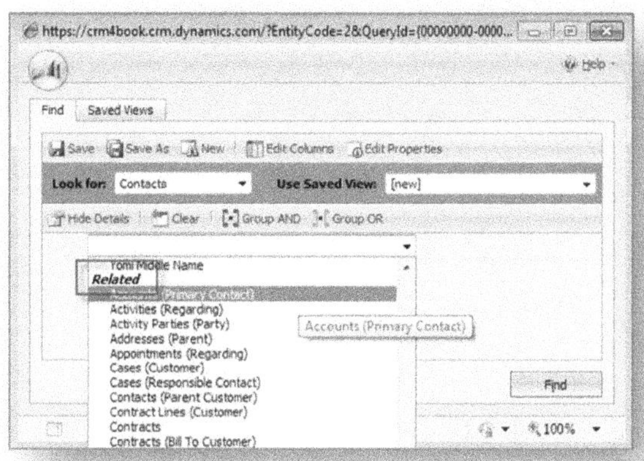

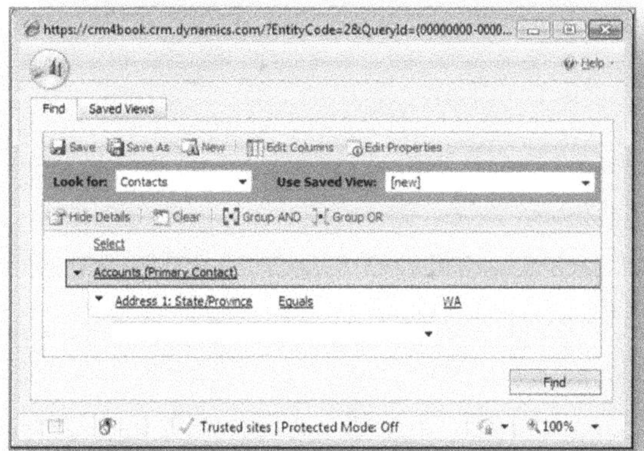

Step-by-Step Instructions

1. Click the Advanced Find button on the toolbar. For this example, let's assume that we are searching for opportunities.
2. Hover your mouse over the Select text. From the drop-down, scroll down the bottom of the list of fields. You'll see related entities. Following the example described above, you could choose Parent Customer (Account) to see a list of fields on the related account record.

Tips & Tricks

- Parent Customer is a term in Microsoft Dynamics CRM that is used whenever a contact or account could be selected. For example, the Parent Customer of a contact could be either an account or contact record.

CHAPTER

7

You've got e-mail!

Configuring Outlook e-mail settings ◆ Installing the CRM e-mail router ◆ Sending a single e-mail from within Outlook ◆ Sending a single e-mail from within CRM ◆ Creating a direct e-mail template ◆ Sending a direct e-mail merge ◆ Sending an e-mail merge using Word ◆ Viewing e-mails attached to CRM records

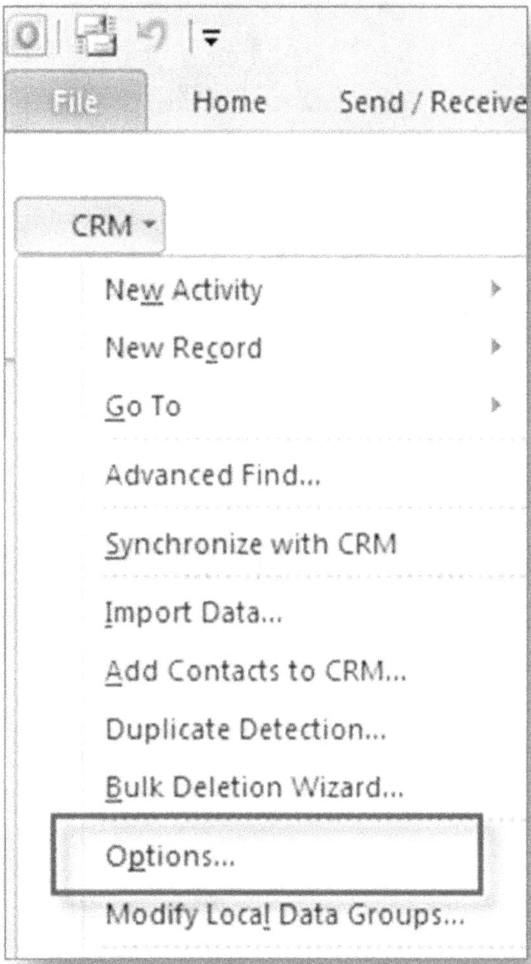

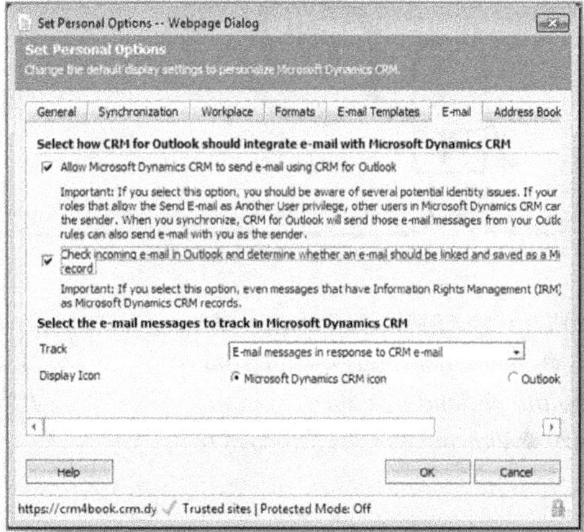

Configuring Outlook e-mail settings

First thing's first: Unless your company has implemented the CRM E-mail Router, you'll need to configure your Outlook to work with CRM.

This will allow Microsoft Dynamics CRM to send e-mails using CRM for Outlook. Why do you have to manually set Outlook to work with CRM for sending e-mail? Because Outlook basically assumes that all plugins are viruses and requires that that you manually give CRM permission to send e-mails through Outlook.

Step-by-Step Instructions

1. Click Add-Ins on the Outlook ribbon and then choose the CRM drop-down.
2. Click Options.
3. Click the E-mail tab.
4. Choose the option to allow CRM e-mails to be sent through Outlook and click OK.

Tips & Tricks

- If you don't allow Outlook to send e-mails on CRM's behalf, you will likely receive multiple annoying pop-up messages when CRM attempts to deliver e-mail messages.
- Each user must individually allow Outlook to send e-mail on behalf of CRM.

Installing the CRM E-mail Router

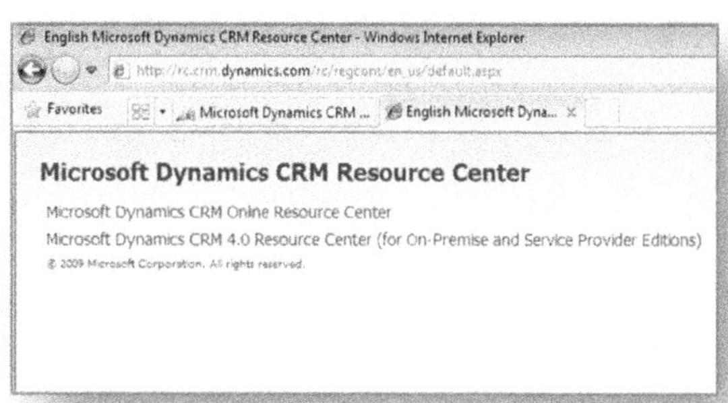

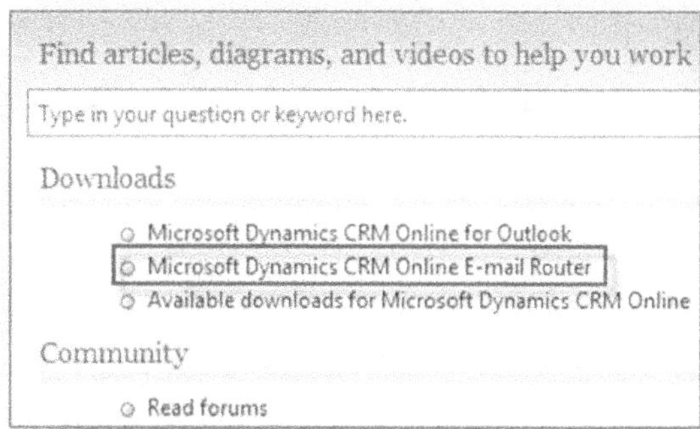

When you send an e-mail in CRM, that e-mail either is delivered through an individual user's Outlook program, or the e-mail is routed to the E-mail Router. This E-mail Router is a separate application that acts as a gateway between CRM and your Exchange/POP/SMTP e-mail server.

You can download the CRM E-mail Router from the Microsoft Dynamics CRM Resource Center.

Step-by-Step Instructions

1. Go to http://rc.crm.dynamics.com/rc and choose either CRM On-Premise or CRM Online.

2. Under Downloads, Click Microsoft Dynamics CRM Online E-mail Router.

3. Click the Download button and follow the installation instructions.

Tips & Tricks

- The location of the download files for the E-mail Router may change. Go a Bing search if the instructions above don't work.

- The CRM E-mail Router only needs to be installed once per database. It will send emails for all of your users.

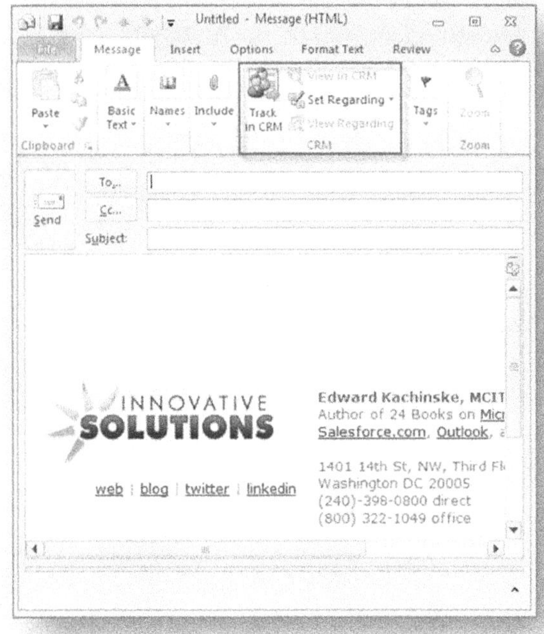

Sending a single e-mail from within Outlook

You can associate any Outlook e-mail (incoming or outgoing) with any record in CRM. If you have an important e-mail, tracking it in CRM will make it available to other CRM users, without sharing your entire Sent Items folder in Outlook.

Tracking e-mails back to records also makes it easier to gain a 360 degree understanding of your company's interactions with a contact or company.

Step-by-Step Instructions

1. Create a new e-mail message in Outlook.

2. (Option 1) Click the Track in CRM button on the ribbon. Assuming the e-mail address for the recipient lines up with a record in CRM, the e-mail will be tracked to the record. (This may be a big assumption.)

3. (Option 2) Click the Set Regarding button if you want to manually associate the e-mail with a record in CRM

Tips & Tricks

- Tracked e-mails appear in the History tab for a record in CRM, alongside other completed activities.

Sending a single e-mail from within CRM

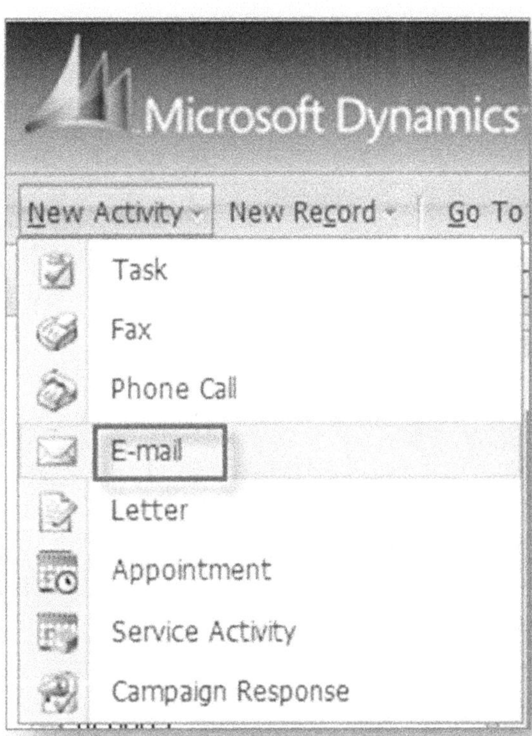

While you send most of your e-mail messages from within Outlook, you may at some point want to send a single e-mail from within CRM. Usually, this happens in cases when you already have a CRM record on the screen.

This way, you won't need to leave CRM to send an email, and it also gives you the opportunity to send e-mails from a computer that doesn't have Outlook on it.

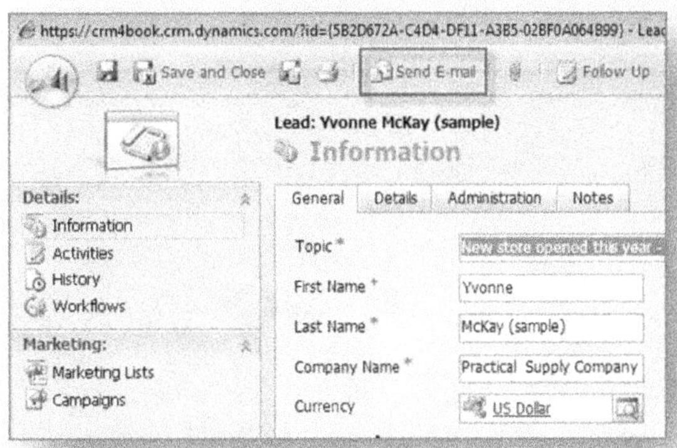

Step-by-Step Instructions

1. (Option 1) Click New Activity on the toolbar, and then choose E-mail.
2. Fill out your e-mail and click Send.
3. (Option 2) Open a contact record and click the Send E-mail button on the toolbar.

Tips & Tricks

- If you send e-mails directly from within CRM, you will need to have configured Outlook to send e-mails on CRM's behalf. Or your organization will need to have the CRM E-mail Router installed.

Creating a direct e-mail template

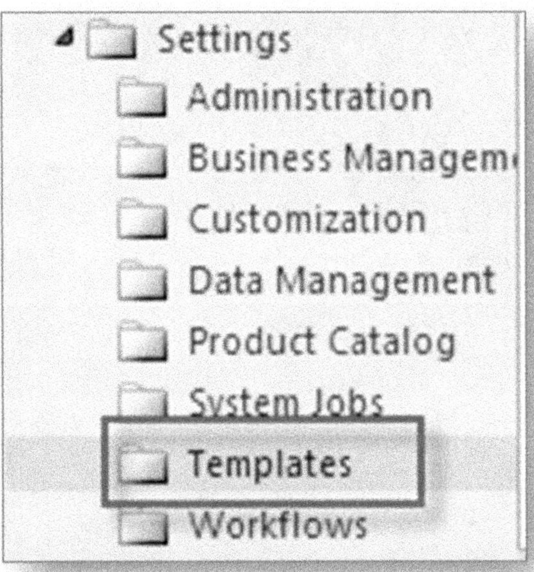

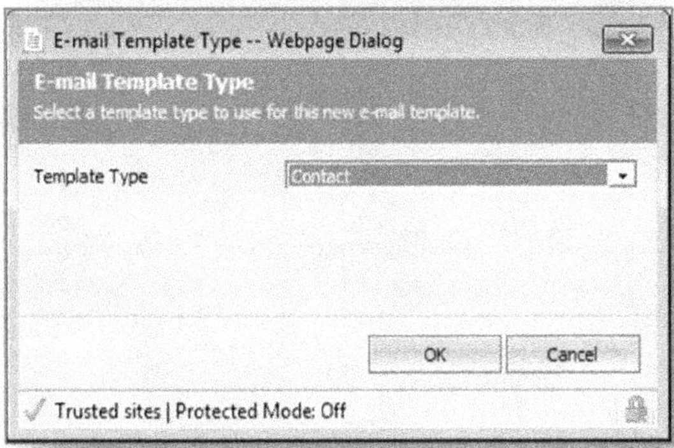

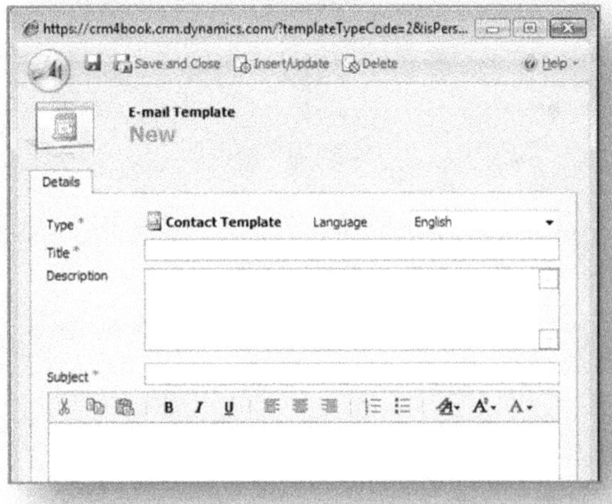

E-mail templates are really useful if you want to send the same e-mail to a bunch of recipients. E-mail templates can be set up and sent out directly in Microsoft Dynamics CRM.

Step-by-Step Instructions

1. Click Settings on the Navigation Pane, and then click Templates.
2. Click E-mail Templates.
3. Click the New button on the Actions toolbar.
4. Select your template type (usually Contact or Account) and click OK.
5. Configure your template and click Save and Close.

Tips & Tricks

- Click the Insert/Update button to insert field placeholders into an e-mail template.
- See the next page for instructions on what to do with e-mail templates once you have created them.
- For a better e-mail system, check out CoreMotives. More information is available at www.coremotives.com.

Sending a direct e-mail merge

Once you have your template ready, you can send an e-mail merge to a single person or a group of recipients directly in CRM.

Sending a direct e-mail is the quickest and easiest way to do an e-mail merge in Microsoft Dynamics CRM. (Other ways include using Workflow and using the Word mail merge feature.)

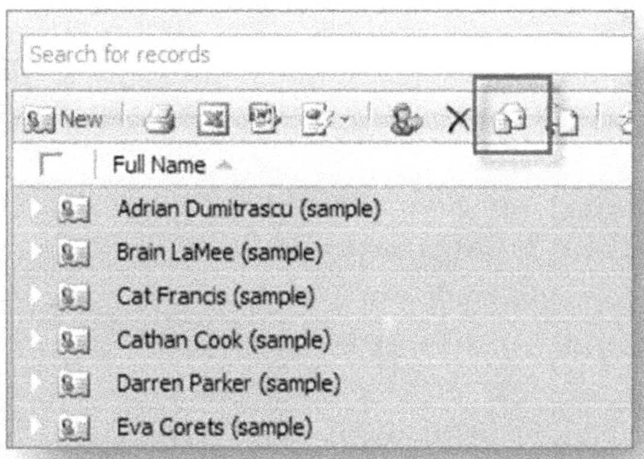

Step-by-Step Instructions

1. Highlight a group of records.
2. Click the Direct E-mail button on the Actions toolbar.
3. Select an e-mail template, select a range of recipients, and click Send. (It's really that easy.)

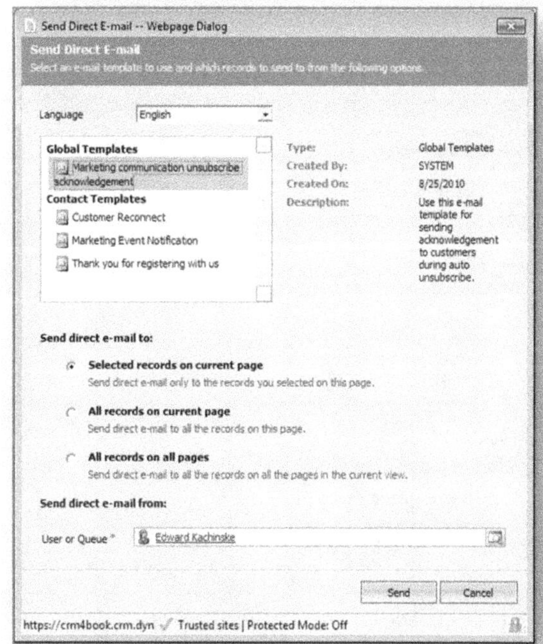

Tips & Tricks

- It's a good idea to send mass e-mails to test group within your company before sending to the general population.
- If you are sending hundreds of emails (or more), then you should use a third party to deliver the messages. Sending through your Exchange server could end up putting your organization on spam blacklists.

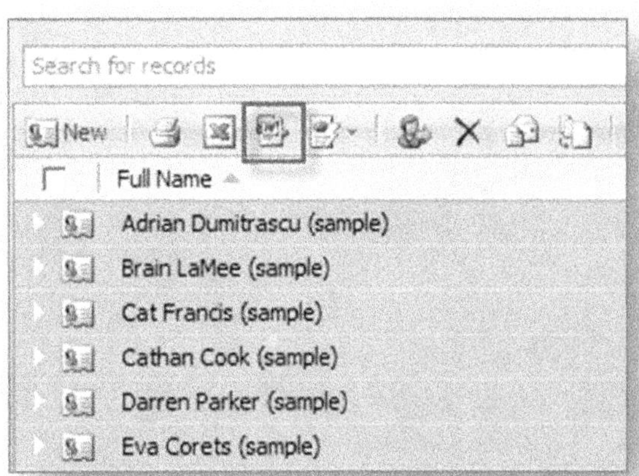

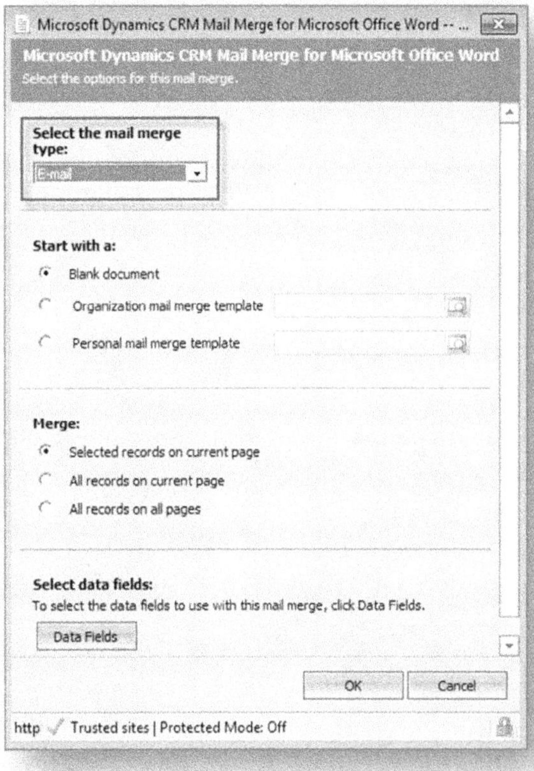

Sending an e-mail merge using Word

So the direct e-mails sent within CRM are text only. If you want to insert fancy graphics, differing text sizes, or other HTML features, you'll need to send the e-mail using Microsoft Office Word.

Though an e-mail merge in word is harder to set up than a direct email (covered on the previous page) in CRM, you'll end up with a much more colorful end product.

Step-by-Step Instructions

1. Highlight a group of records.
2. Click the Word button on the Actions Toolbar.
3. From the mail merge type drop-down, choose E-mail. Select a range of recipient records, and click OK.
4. Click Open to open the Word Document. Follow the instructions on-screen to create a template. The last step in the Word mail merge wizard will allow you to send the mail merge to e-mail recipients.

Tips & Tricks

- You cannot attach files to e-mails sent through this process. If you need to attach files, consider uploading them to a server and then reference them with a hyperlink.

Viewing e-mails attached to CRM records

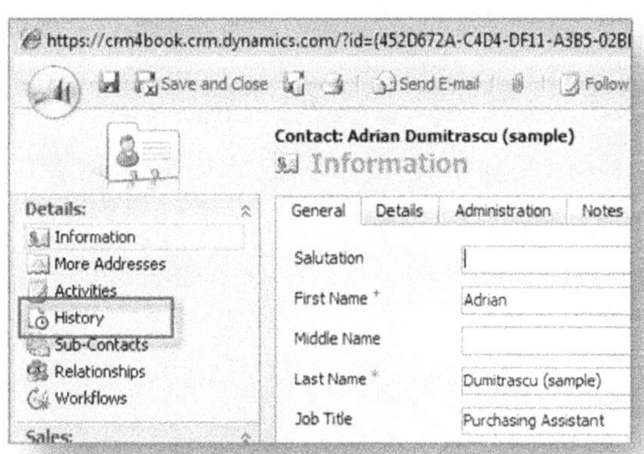

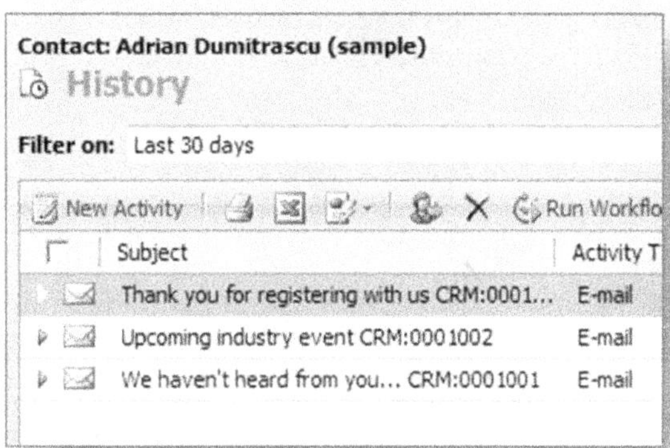

Once you've tracked an Outlook e-mail in CRM, you can view that e-mail under the associated record's history. E-mails that are sent directly in CRM can also be viewed under a record's history.

Tracking e-mails, of course, does have disadvantages. For example, if all of your messages are tracked, your boss will know whether or not you have been e-mailing prospects on a regular basis.

Step-by-Step Instructions

1. Open a record.
2. On the left, click History.
3. In the date range drop-down, select a range of dates for history entries. The default only shows history entries for the last 30 days.
4. Double-click an e-mail history to open it.

Tips & Tricks

- Attachments to e-mails will likely be available on history entries. Open a history record, and then click the Attachments tab to see any files that were originally attached to the e-mail message.

CHAPTER

8

Accessing your database in the supermarket aisle using CRM Mobile Express

Configuring CRM Mobile Express ◆ Accessing the database from your mobile phone

Configuring CRM Mobile Express

You can access your database anywhere, at any time using CRM Mobile Express. CRM Mobile Express is a CRM application that works on your cell phone. With CRM Mobile Express, you won't have any excuse to have a personal life. You can work all the time.

By configuring CRM Mobile Express, you will be able to customize which entities and forms show up when you access your CRM database from your phone.

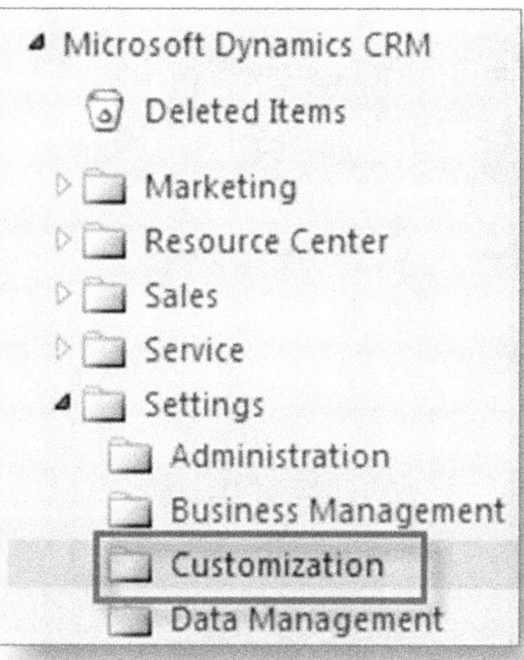

Step-by-Step Instructions

1. Click Settings on the Navigation Pane, and then click Customization.
2. Click Customize Mobile Express.
3. Add any entities that you want to show up in CRM Mobile Express. Click Publish All when you are done.

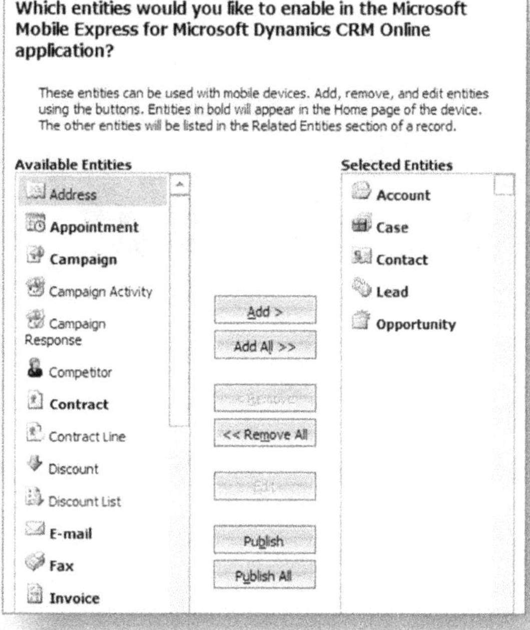

Tips & Tricks

➢ CRM Mobile Express is compatible with most current smartphones. iPhone, Palm Pre, Android, and just about any phone that has a finger push-screen will work with Mobile Express.

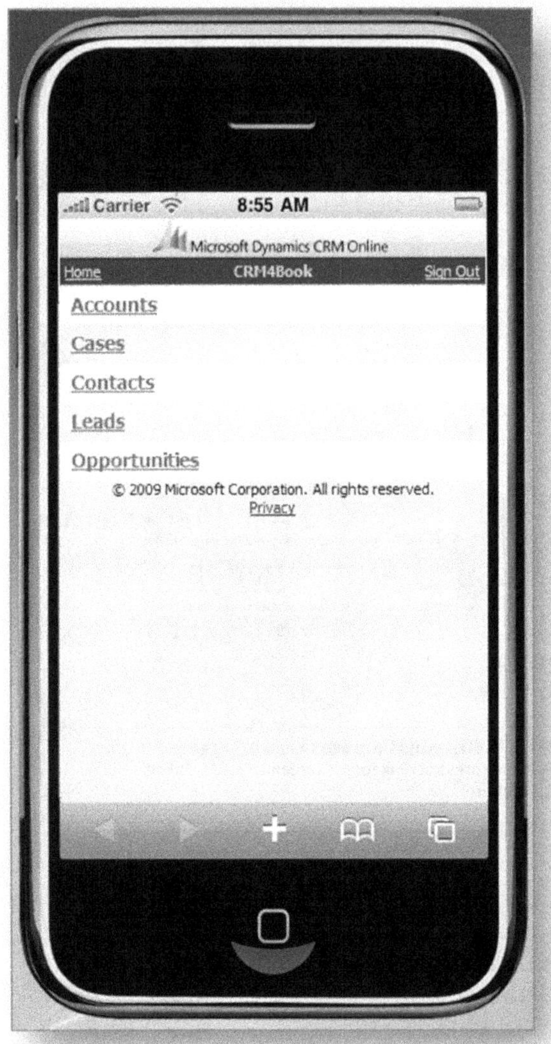

Accessing the database from your mobile phone

I'm sure you've thought to yourself, "I don't spend enough time working." Well, now you can access your database from the supermarket check-out line using CRM Mobile Express.

CRM Mobile Express is accessed in the browser of your cell phone. Basically, you just open a web browser on your phone and direct it to go to the URL for your database.

Step-by-Step Instructions

1. Open the browser on your phone.
2. Type your CRM database URL into the address bar.
3. Log in to your database with your Windows Live ID and password.

Tips & Tricks

- Many Blackberry devices still don't support JavaScript, and if you have one of these devices, you may still be able to access your database using a third party application.

CHAPTER

9

Working with Leads (aka turning strangers into buyers)

Entering a new lead ◆ Qualifying a lead ◆ Disqualifying a lead

Entering a new lead

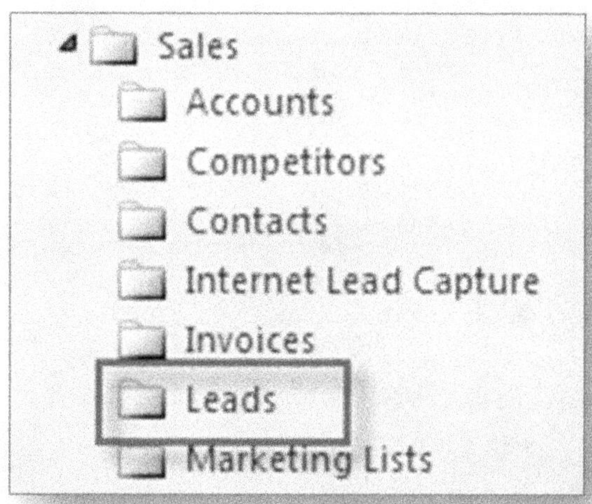

A lead is a potential customer that you have not qualified yet. Think of leads as people on a spreadsheet, business cards left in a punchbowl at a conference. They're people without faces.

Once you know that the potential customer (1) has a pulse and (2) has expressed some interest in purchasing your product/service, then you should convert the person to a contact with a pending opportunity.

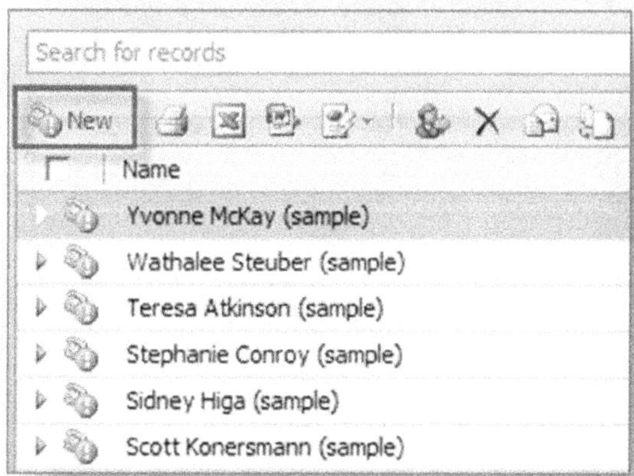

Step-by-Step Instructions

1. Click Sales on the Navigation pane, and then click Leads.

2. Click the New button on the Actions toolbar.

3. Enter information about the lead. Click the Save and Close button.

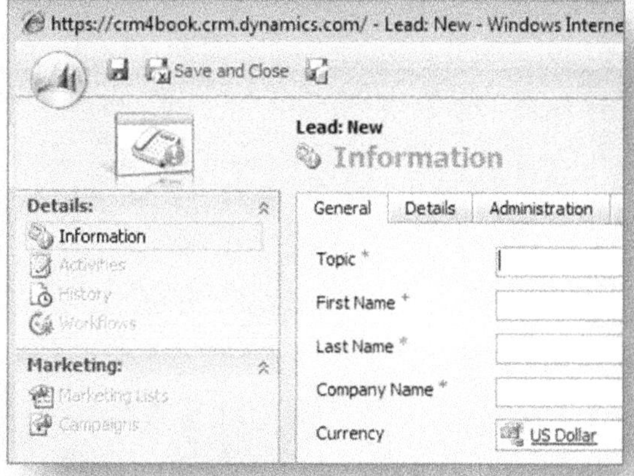

Tips & Tricks

- Notes entered on a lead record will not transfer to a contact record when the lead is qualified. So if you are engaged enough with a lead to make notes, then it's time to convert the record to a contact.

- You may want to enter new contacts as leads and then convert them to contacts immediately. This way, you can enter information about the contact, company, and a pending opportunity all on one screen. This is generally easier than creating a separate company, contact, and opportunity record.

Qualifying a lead

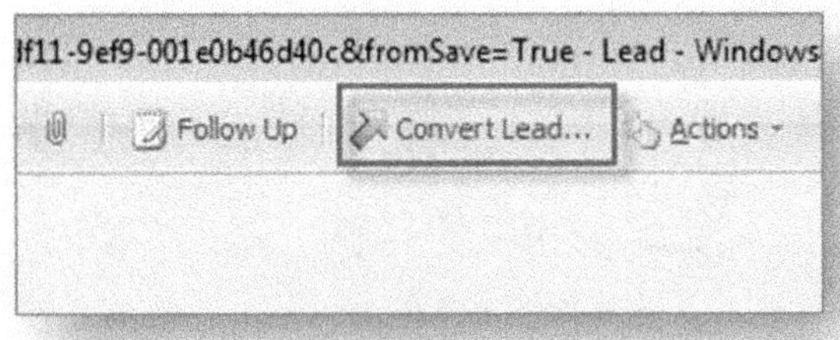

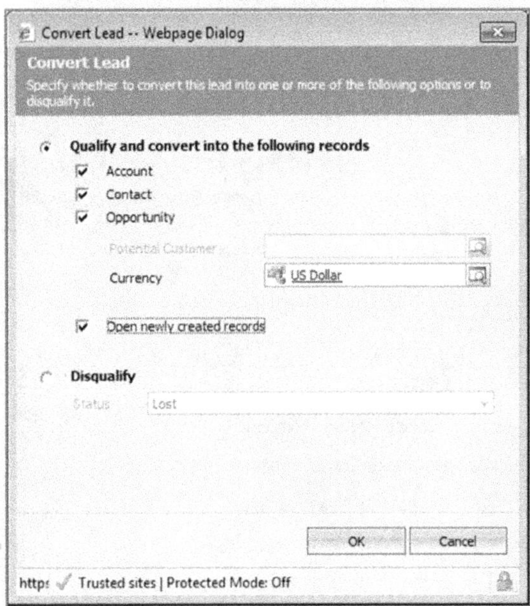

A lead shouldn't remain a lead for long. Playing hard to get does not usually work very well in the sales world, so you will want to qualify a lead quickly.

As soon as you have made any kind of positive contact with a lead, you should convert it to a contact with an open opportunity.

Step-by-Step Instructions

1. Click Sales on the Navigation Pane, and then click Leads.
2. Double click the lead that you want to qualify.
3. Click the Convert Lead button.
4. Choose the Qualify option and click the option to create an Account, Contact, and Opportunity.
5. Click OK.

Tips & Tricks

- When a lead is qualified, the original lead record is deactivated and data from the lead is transferred to new account, contact, and opportunity records.
- When qualifying a lead, it might be a good idea to click the option to open the newly created contact, account, or opportunity records.

Disqualifying a lead

Sometimes leads don't work out, and that's OK. It's nothing you should take personally. Just disqualify that lead and move on. There are plenty of other fish in the sea.

A disqualified lead remains in the system, but not in your active views. If the customer ever re-surfaces, you can always re-activate the record.

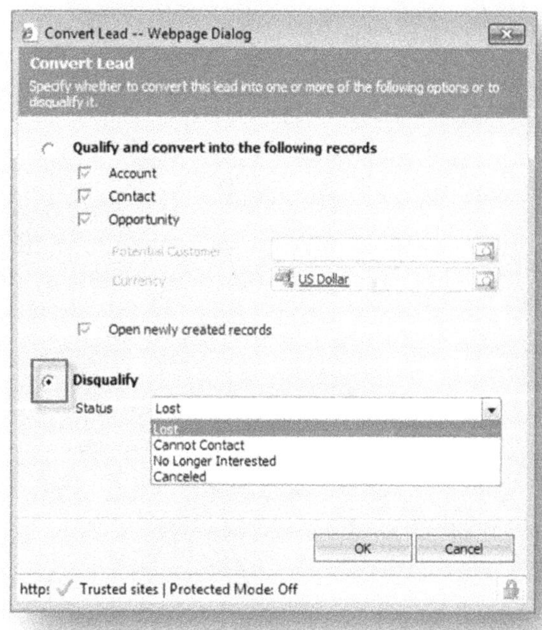

Step-by-Step Instructions

1. Click Sales on the Navigation Pane, and then click Leads.
2. Double-click a lead.
3. Click the Convert Lead button on the toolbar.
4. Select the Disqualify option.
5. Click OK.

Tips & Tricks

- Disqualified records are automatically deactivated.
- To see a list of disqualified records, go to the Leads view and choose the Inactive Records view from the View drop-down in the upper right corner of the view.

CHAPTER

10

Managing the product catalog (it's harder than you think)

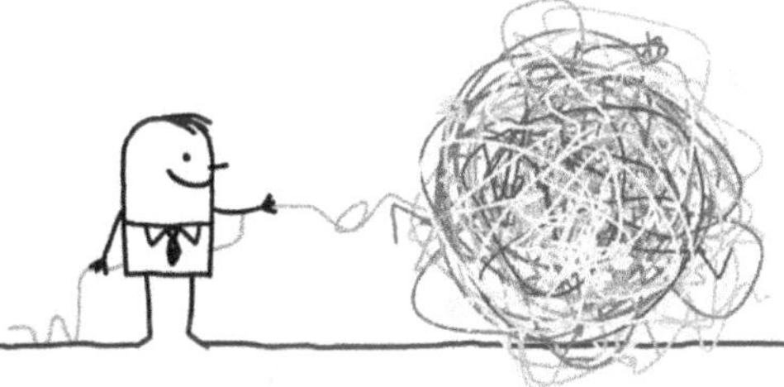

Creating unit groups ◆ Creating price lists ◆ Adding products to the product catalog ◆ Managing discount lists

Creating unit groups

You're probably selling something, right? Fortunately, the product catalog in Microsoft Dynamics CRM can help you streamline the sales process and customize it for you or your business.

First you'll need to create unit groups. These are the units of whatever you are selling. Hours, for example, might be the unit that a service company works with. If you sell soda, your unit groups might be cans and cases.

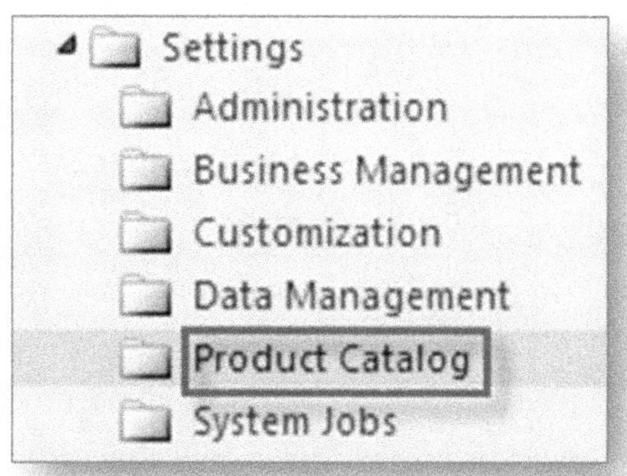

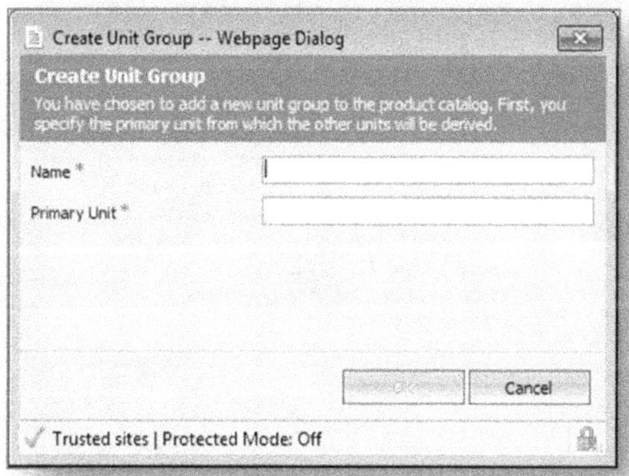

Step-by-Step Instructions

1. Click Settings on the Navigation Pane, and then click Product Catalog.
2. Click Unit Groups.
3. Click the New button.
4. Enter in a name and primary unit.
5. Click Save and Close.

Tips & Tricks

- If you are selling soda, you might have multiple unit groups. You might sell pallets, cases, and bottles of soda. Each could be units within a unit group.

Creating price lists

Once you have a unit group set up, you can create a price list. This list will help you determine and keep track of different prices for different customers.

You might, for instance, charge a different price for students, senior citizens, or government agencies. A price list can allow you to set different prices for different quantities of your product.

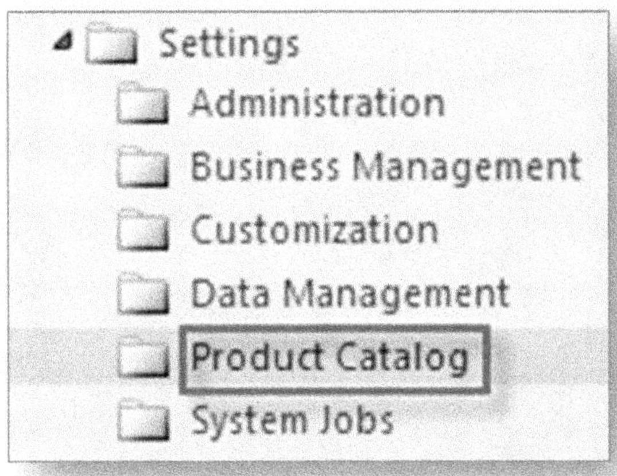

Price Lists

A price list specifies what prices can be charged for each unit in the unit group of a product. In this section, you create, manage, and delete price list line items and price lists in the product catalog. You associate and disassociate products with price lists. You also specify various pricing options in the price list line items, such as the quantity selling option, the pricing method, and the rounding options.

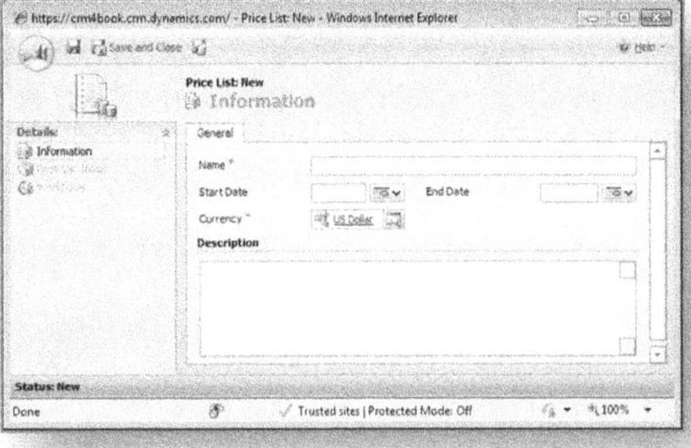

Step-by-Step Instructions

1. Click Settings on the Navigation Pane, and then click Product Catalog.
2. Click Price Lists.
3. Click the New button.
4. Give your price list a name and click Save.
5. Click Add Price List Item.
6. Enter in information about the item and click Save and Close.

Tips & Tricks

- Each product sold using CRM's product catalog will need to have a price associated with each price list.
- When you create a new opportunity, you'll have to specify a price list for the opportunity, and then when you add products to the opportunity, the customer's cost will be determined by the price list.

Adding products to the product catalog

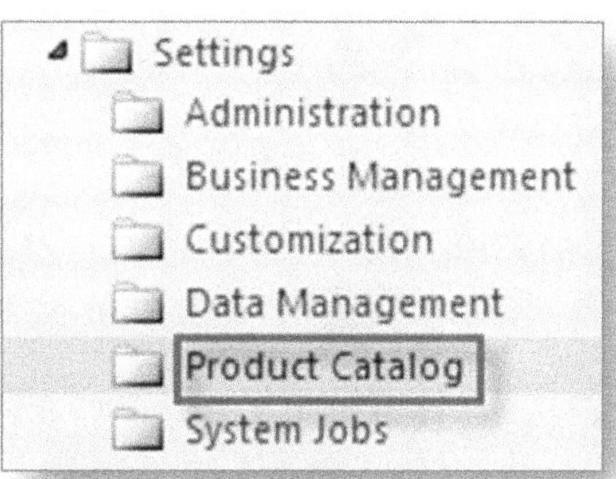

You can't have a product catalog without products, so you'll need to know how to add products to you product catalog.

Managing your product catalog can be a little tricky, so just remember that the products in your product catalog are essentially just items that you sell.

Products

A product is an item in the product catalog that you want to sell to your accounts. In this section, you add new products to and modify information for existing products in the product catalog. You activate or deactivate products, and also reclassify them to move them to other areas of the product catalog (and subject tree).

Step-by-Step Instructions

1. Click Settings in the Navigation Pane, and then click Product Catalog.

2. Click Products.

3. Click the New button.

4. Enter in information about your product. Select a unit group and a default unit.

4. Click Save. In the details area, select the price list items associated with this product.

6. Click Save and Close.

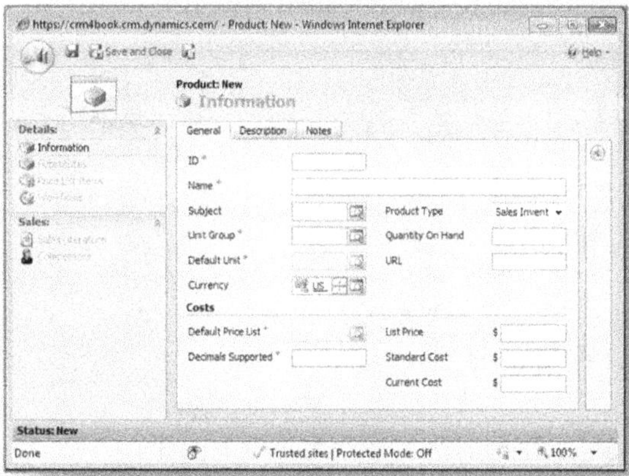

Tips & Tricks

- Each product in the product list needs to have prices specified at each price list.

- If your opportunity process is fairly simple and doesn't involve huge inventory, using the product catalog might be overkill.

Managing discount lists

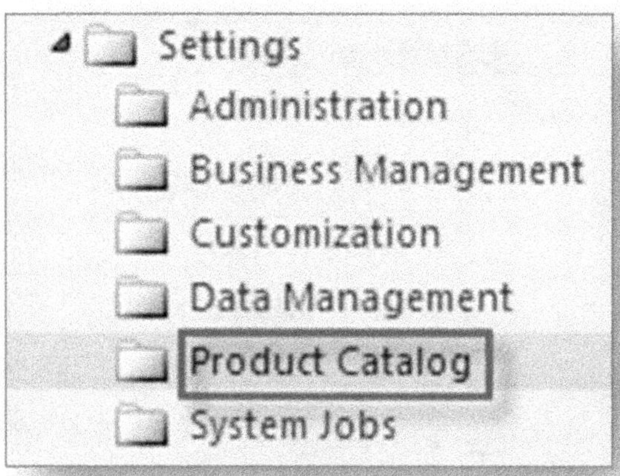

Discount Lists

A discount list contains the specific discounts that can be applied to a product, based on volume purchased. In this section, you create, manage, and delete discount lists in the product catalog.

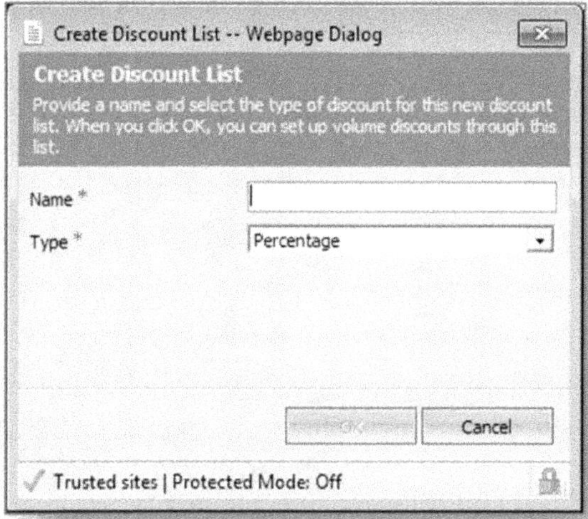

People are always looking to save money, so it would be really hard to sell a product if you never offered discounts.

Microsoft Dynamics CRM helps you keep track of the various discounts on your products with discount lists. You could have a senior citizen discount, a returning customer discount, or a discount associated with a specific promotion or discount code.

Step-by-Step Instructions

1. Click Settings on the Navigation Pane, and then click Product Catalog.
2. Click Discount Lists.
3. Click the New button.
4. Give your list a name and choose amount or percentage discount.
5. On the left, click Discounts.
6. Click New Discounts.
7. Enter in information about your discount.
8. Click Save and Close.

Tips & Tricks

- You can restrict the opportunity screens so that products can only be discounted by these pre-defined discounts.

CHAPTER 11

When are you going to get around to selling? (opportunities)

Entering a new opportunity ◆ Associating products with opportunities ◆ Defining your competitors on an opportunity ◆ Adding sales literature to an opportunity ◆ Organizing your opportunities ◆ Closing a won or lost opportunity

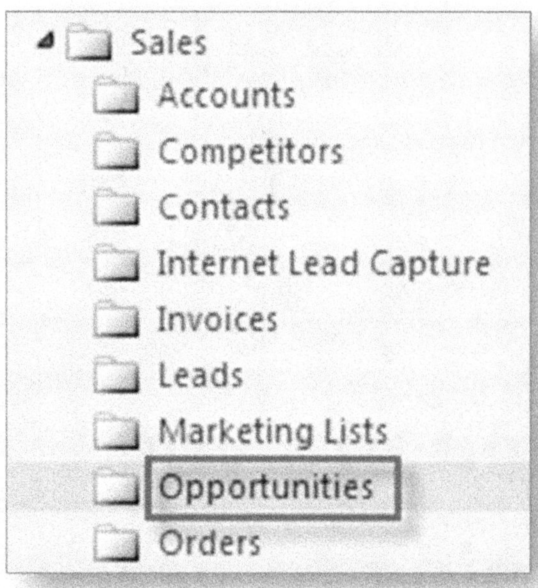

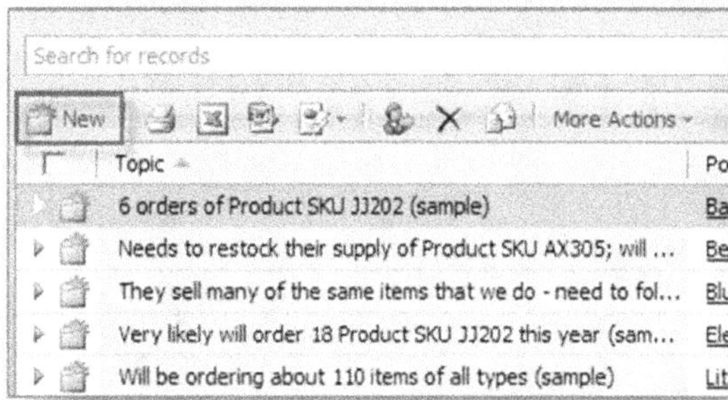

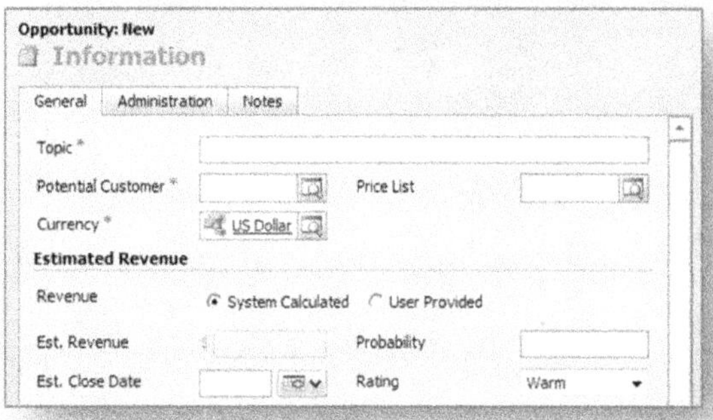

Entering a new opportunity

So you've found potential sale? Good for you! You'll want to enter the potential sale into your database as an opportunity.

An opportunity is a record that contains information about a sale with a contact or account in your system.

Step-by-Step Instructions

1. Click Sales on the Navigation Pane, and then click Opportunities.
2. Click the New button on the toolbar.
3. Enter information about your opportunity and click Save and Close.

Tips & Tricks

➢ When creating a new opportunity, you can add products from the product catalog by clicking the Products option on the left.

➢ An opportunity's dollar value can be automatically calculated based on the products selected and the price list chosen. Or, you can manually write-in a dollar amount.

Associating products with opportunities

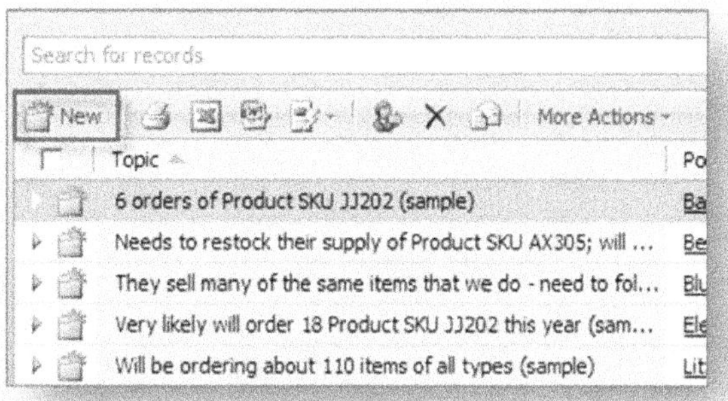

Unless you skipped over Chapter 9, you know how to set up and manage you catalog. If you did skip it over, you might want to go back before reading this page.

Products in your product catalog can be associated with opportunities in your database, which helps you do important things like calculate potential revenue and create quotes. Plus, any product data that you add to an opportunity will transfer over to quotes, orders, and invoices.

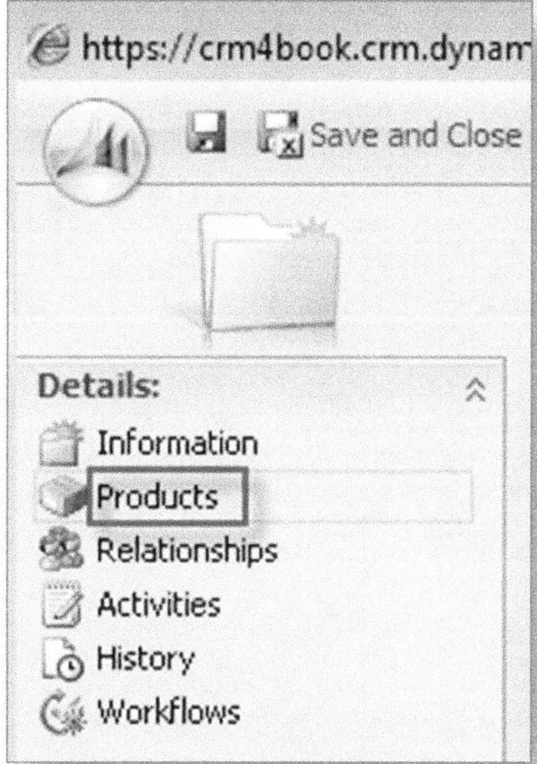

Step-by-Step Instructions

1. Create or open an opportunity.
2. On the left, click Products.
3. Click the New Opportunity Product button.
4. Select a product, unit, and quantity.
5. Click Save and Close.

Tips & Tricks

- You must select a Price List on the opportunity before you can add any products to the opportunity.
- Pricing for products added to an opportunity will be calculated based on the price for the selected Price List.

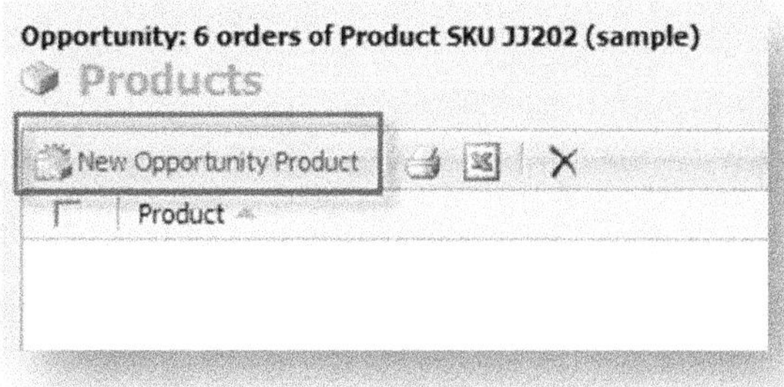

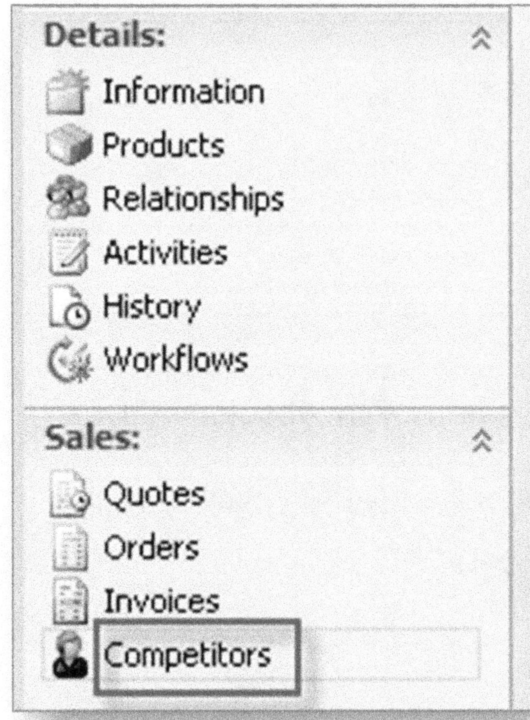

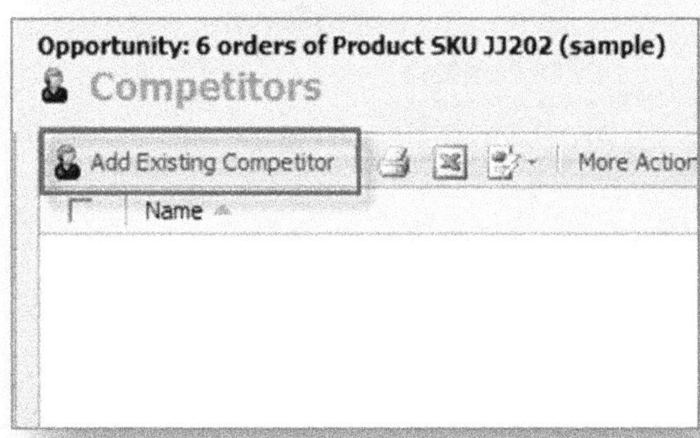

Defining your competitors on an opportunity

Keep your friends close and your enemies closer. Understanding your competition is an important part of sales and marketing, and with Microsoft Dynamics CRM, you can manage a list of competitors that will allow you to stay on top who you are winning (or losing) against.

Associate a competitor to an opportunity when find out that you are competing with a competitor for that opportunity.

Step-by-Step Instructions

1. Create or open an opportunity.
2. Click Competitors on the left.
3. Click Add Existing Competitor on the Actions Toolbar.
4. Highlight the competitor and click OK.
5. Click Save and Close.

Tips & Tricks

- When you close an opportunity, you'll also have the opportunity to select the competitor that you won/lost against.

Adding Sales Literature

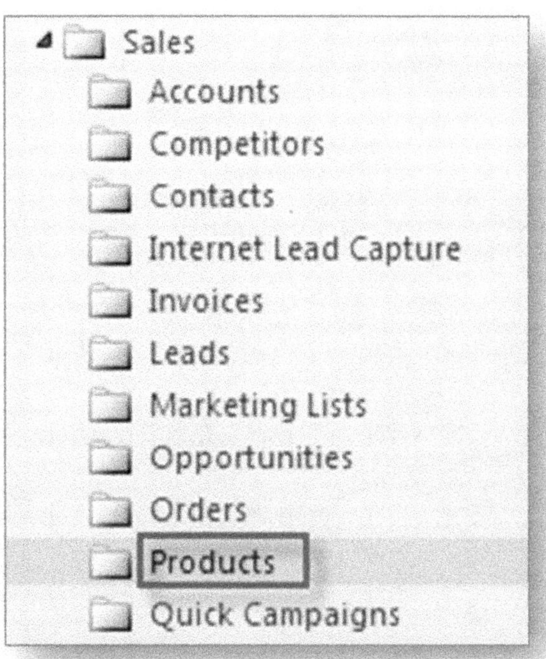

Leaflets, sales slicks, price lists, galore! Keep this stuff handy in the Sales Literature feature, and you'll never have to go hunting for that price list again.

Sales literature can be associated with any product, and associating your sales literature will make easy for your salespeople to bring up product-specific documentation.

Step-by-Step Instructions

1. Click Sales on the Navigation Pane, and then click Products.
2. Open an existing product or click the New button to create a new product.
3. On the left, click Sales Literature.
4. Click the New/Add buttons on the Actions toolbar to link sales literature to this product.

Tips & Tricks

- If you need more complex document management, consider integrating Sharepoint into your CRM database.

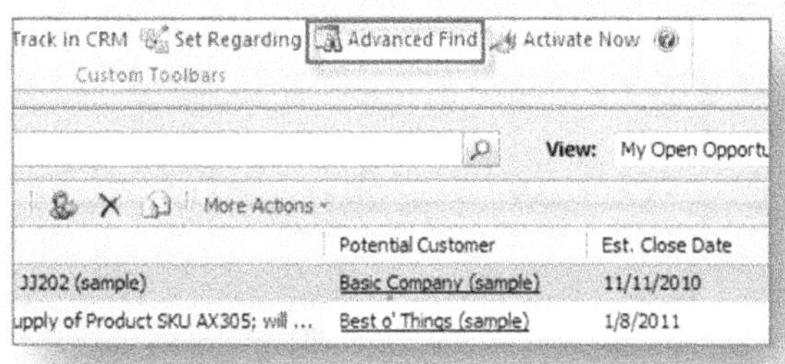

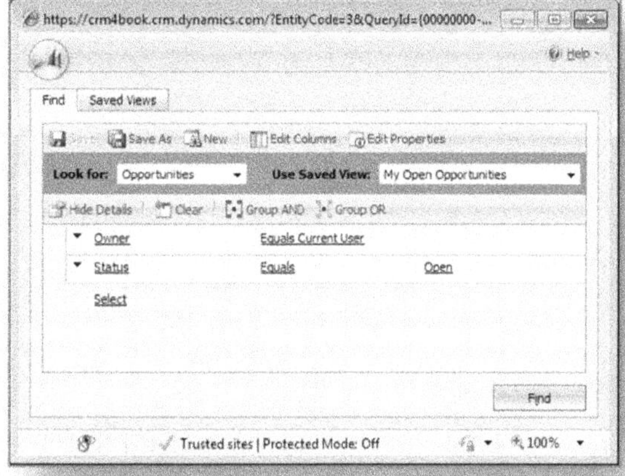

Organizing your opportunities

Opportunities can be hard to manage, especially if you have a lot of them. They are also an essential part of the sales process, so you will want to come up with a way to organize them so that you don't have this huge overwhelming list of opportunities to deal with.

You can get around this problem by creating views of certain opportunities. This way, you can have different views to view different types of opportunities.

Step-by-Step Instructions

1. Click Sales on the Navigation Pane, and then click Opportunities.
2. Click the Advanced Find button on the toolbar.
3. Configure your Advanced Find to search for a subset of your opportunities.
4. Click the Edit Columns button to configure the columns that will appear in your view
5. Click the Save As button to save your Advanced Find as a view on the opportunity screen.

Tips & Tricks

- Check out the Search chapter of this book for more information on the Advanced Find feature.

Closing a won or lost opportunity

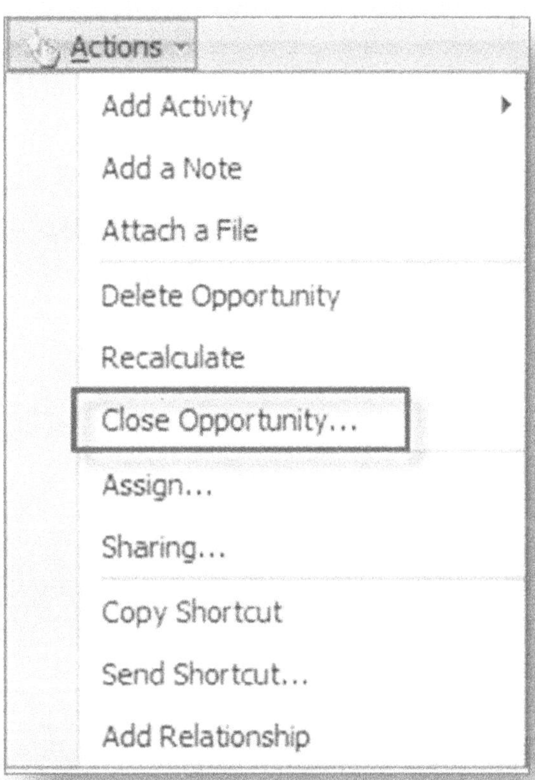

Eventually you will either win or lose a sales opportunity. When this time comes, you will want to close the won or lost opportunity.

Opportunities are no longer active once they have been closed and do not appear with your active contacts. But fear not! Any close/lost opportunity can be reactivated if the customer comes back.

Step-by-Step Instructions

1. Double-click an opportunity in the opportunity list view.
2. Click the Actions drop-down, then Close Opportunity.
3. Define the opportunity as won or lost and choose a reason for the end of the opportunity.
4. Enter in any other important information.
5. Click OK.

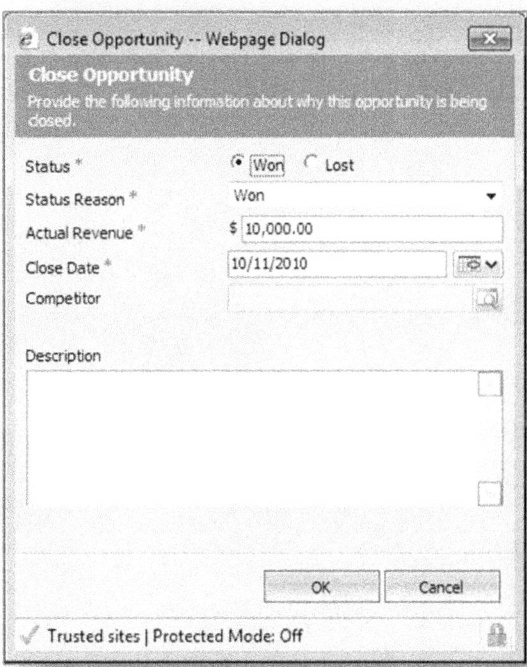

Tips & Tricks

- For sales reports that show won/lost/inactive opportunities, consider creating a pivot table in Excel.

CHAPTER

12

It's about time you sold something: Quotes, Orders, and Invoices

Creating a quote from an opportunity ◆ Modifying pricing and products on a quote ◆ Activating a quote ◆ Printing a quote ◆ Generating an order from a quote ◆ Generating an invoice from an order

Creating a quote from an opportunity

So an opportunity is finally interested in your product? The next step in the sales process involves sending a quote to the potential customer.

Quotes in Microsoft Dynamics CRM are automatically generated as a Word Document.

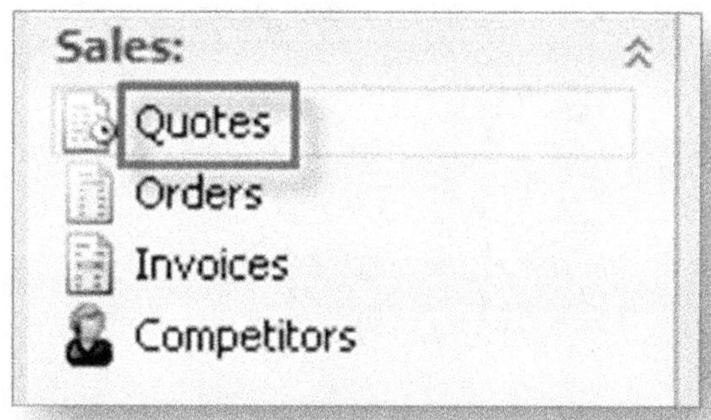

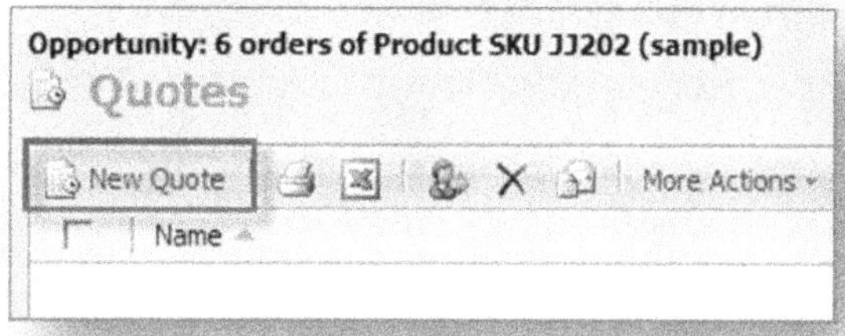

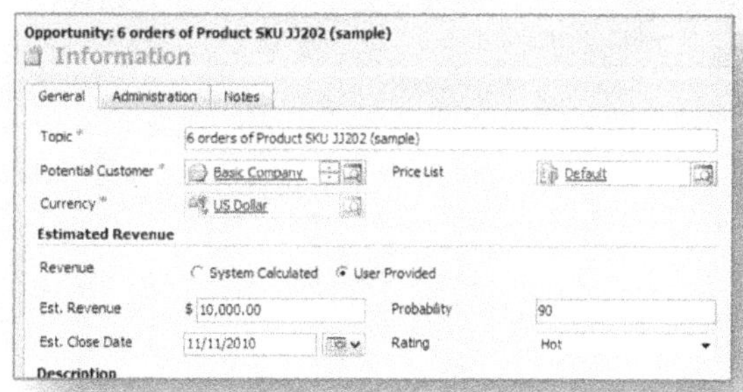

Step-by-Step Instructions

1. Open an existing opportunity.
2. Click Quotes on the left.
3. Click New Quote on the Actions Toolbar.
4. Make sure the sales information is correct. (It will pull product information from the opportunity into this quote.
5. Click Save and Close.

Tips & Tricks

- For advanced quoting with CRM 4.0, check out Experlogix. www.experlogix.com

Modifying pricing and products on a quote

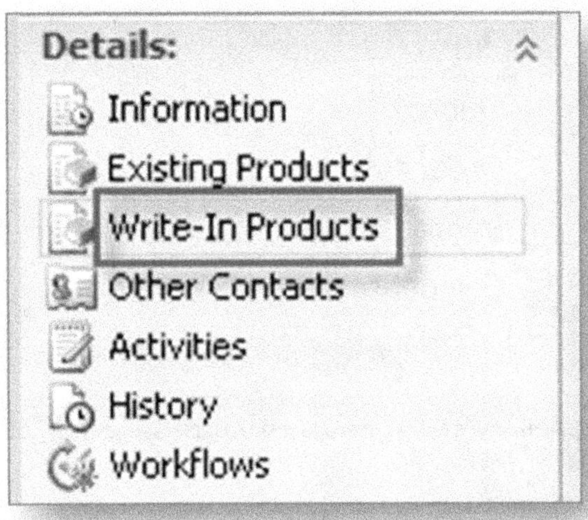

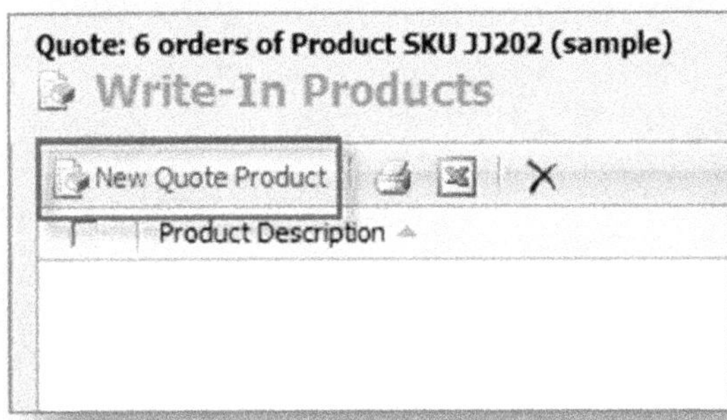

When you create a quote, you are given the option to modify the pricing and products on the quote. You might, for example, want to enter in extra products or change the pricing of a product in your quote.

These changes will show up in the quote but not the parent opportunity.

Step-by-Step Instructions

1. Create a new quote from an opportunity.
2. Save the quote.
3. On the left, click the Write in Products option.
4. Enter in your pricing and product information.
5. Click Save and Close.

Tips & Tricks

- If you have complex quoting requirements, you may need to do much of your quoting in your accounting system. Links to Quickbooks, Microsoft Dynamics GP, Microsoft Dynamics NAV, and others are all available. (And the Microsoft ones are generally free!)

Activating a quote

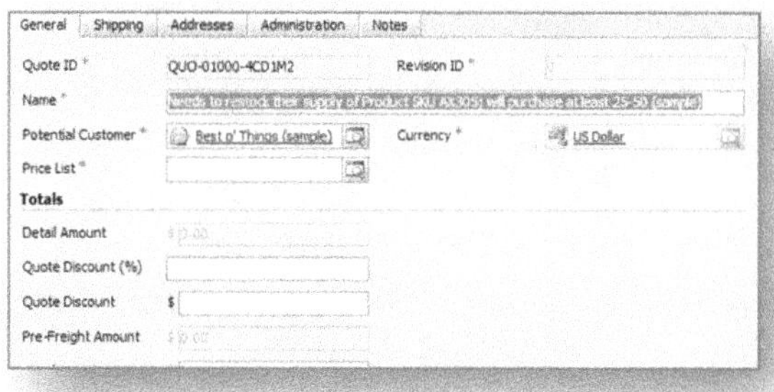

Have you created and modified your quote to your liking? Before you send it off to a customer, you will want to activate your quote.

Once activated, the quote will be set to read-only in the system. If you need to change anything in the quote after you've reactivated it, you should create a new quote from the opportunity.

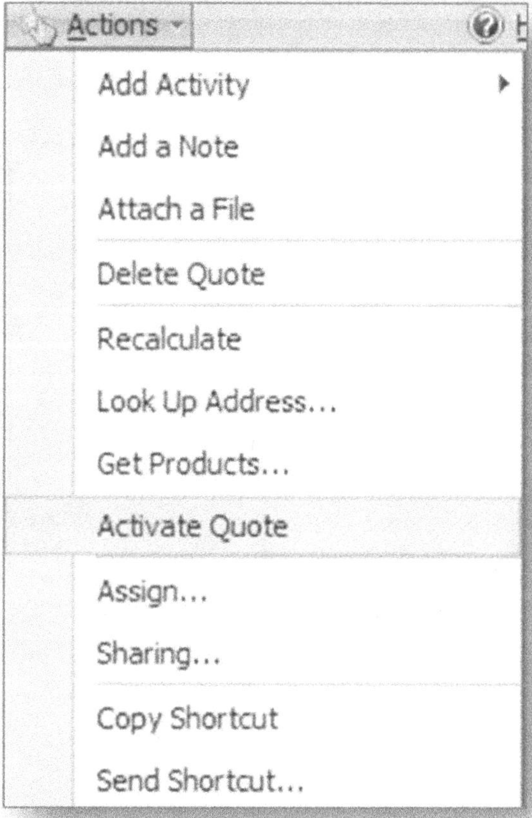

Step-by-Step Instructions

1. Open a quote.
2. Click the Actions button on the toolbar, then Activate Quote.

Tips & Tricks

- Invoices can only be generated from an activated quote.
- You should activate your quote before you print it. (Instructions for printing the quote are on the next page.)

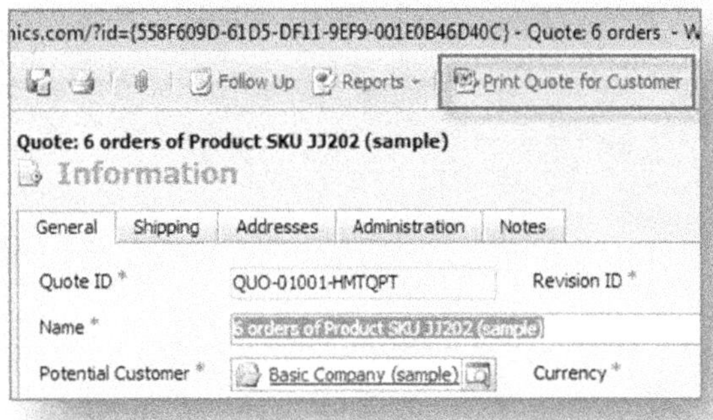

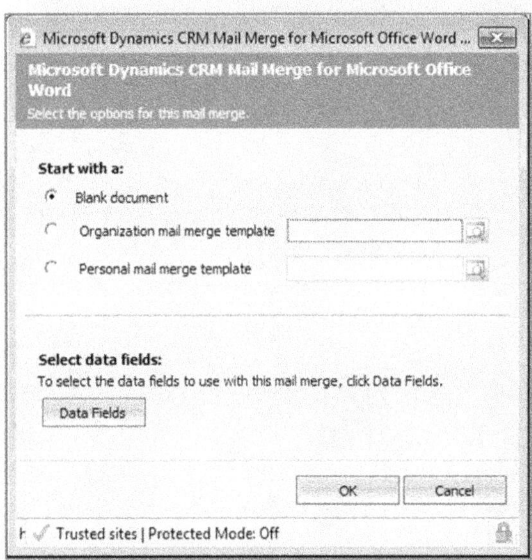

Printing a quote

Once you have made sure that all of the information in your quote is correct, you'll want to print it. Quotes in Microsoft Dynamics CRM are automatically generated as a Word document

Step-by-Step Instructions

1. Create a quote for an opportunity.
2. Click Print Quote for Customer on the toolbar.
3. A Word document will open. Verify the information and print the document.

Tips & Tricks

- You may want to edit the template that CRM uses for quotes. Go to Settings | Templates to see the mail merge templates that can be edited.
- In Word 2010, you can save the Word document directly as a PDF file, which is useful if you don't want the customer to be able to edit the quote.

Generating an order from a quote

So a customer has received your quote and decided to buy your product. You're almost there. The heavy lifting has been done, and you now have to fulfill the order.

In CRM, you can generate an order from any activated quote. Creating an order shows the system that your customer has accepted the quote, and it will tell your fulfillment department that there is an order ready to ship.

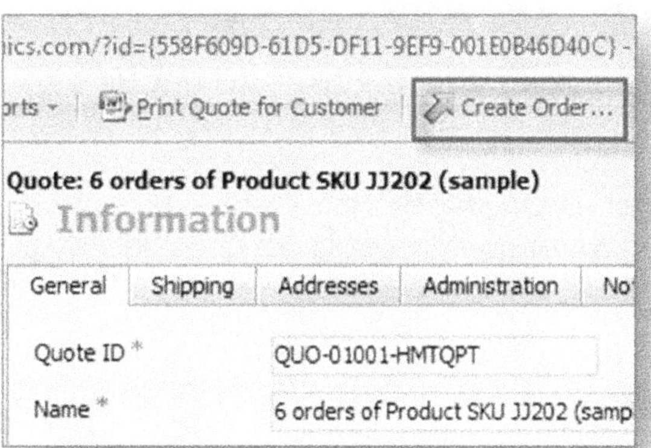

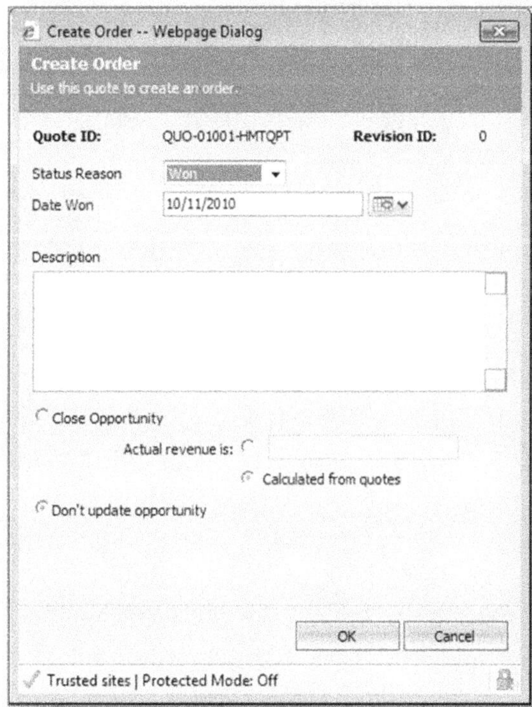

Step-by-Step Instructions

1. Open a quote.
2. Click Actions and then choose Activate Quote.
3. Click the Create Order button on the toolbar..

Tips & Tricks

- Once you create an order for a quote, you should go back and close your originating opportunity. Mark it as having been won.

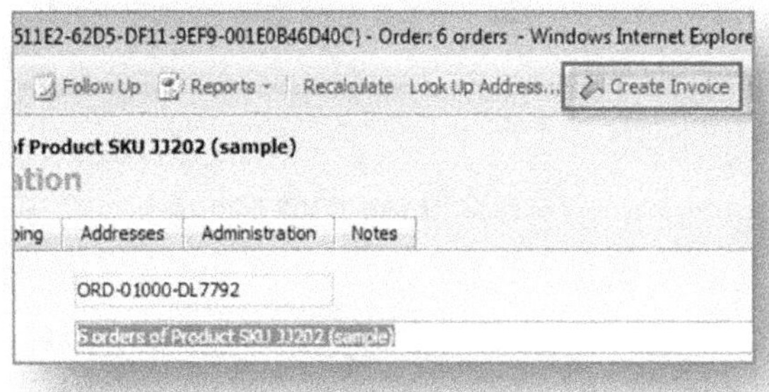

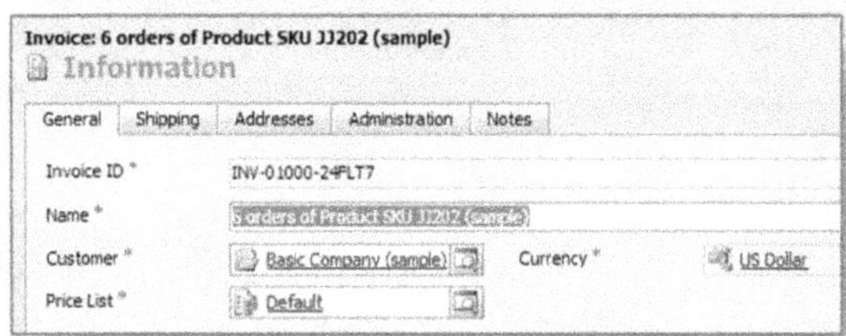

Generating an invoice from an order

Hang in there, because there's one last step in the opportunities / quotes / orders / invoices process. Your customer will need an invoice from you once an order is placed.

This feature is really only useful if CRM is automatically integrated into your accounting system.

Step-by-Step Instructions

1. Open an order.
2. Click the Create Invoice button on the toolbar.

Tips & Tricks

- If your CRM system is not integrated into your accounting system, then you may set up a workflow to automatically send your accounting department an e-mail whenever an invoice is created in CRM. This way, they'll know to send the customer a bill.

CHAPTER

13

Two groups are better than one: marketing lists

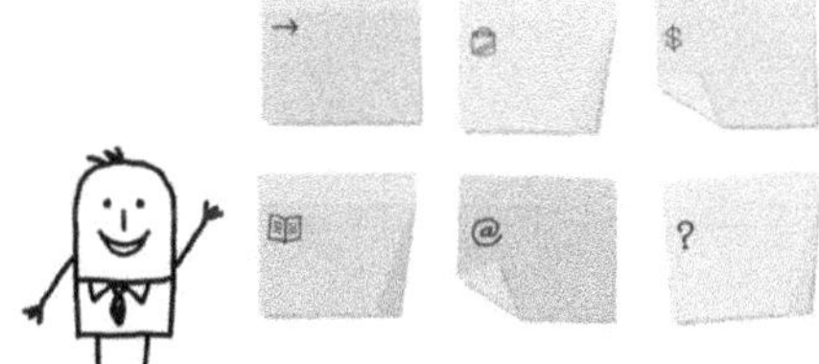

Creating a marketing list ◆ Adding members from a list view ◆ Using lookup or Advanced Find to add members ◆ Using advanced find to remove or evaluate members ◆ Modifying the list membership view ◆ Viewing marketing list information for a single record

Creating a marketing list

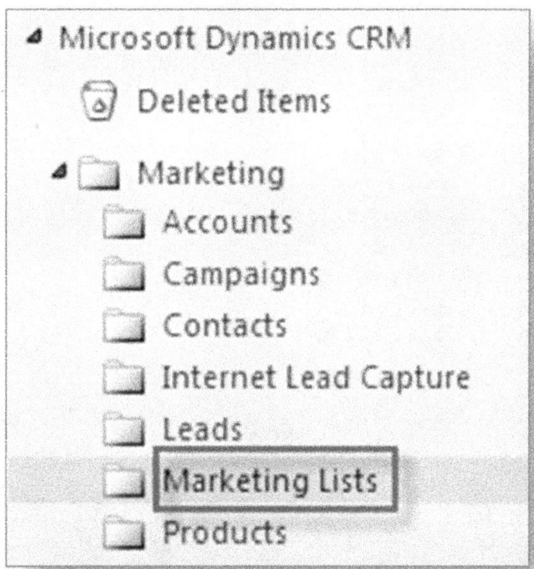

It's time to learn how you can use Microsoft Dynamics CRM to convince your potential customers that they should buy from you.

Before you begin marketing, you will want to create marketing lists so that you can target specific groups of records with campaigns.

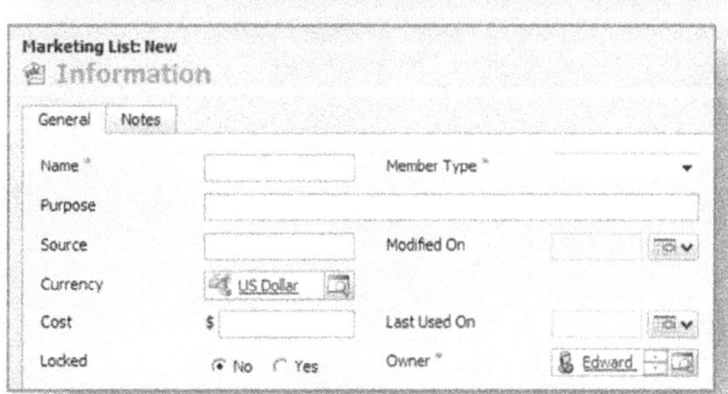

Step-by-Step Instructions

1. Click Marketing on the Navigation Pane, and then click Marketing Lists.

2. Click the New button on the Actions Toolbar.

3. Name your marketing list. Then choose a member type (either contact, account, or lead) and add any other important information.

4. Click Save and Close

Tips & Tricks

- Marketing lists can be made up of either contacts, accounts, or leads. If you need a marketing list that has both contacts and leads, for example, you'd have to create two separate marketing lists.

Adding members from a list view

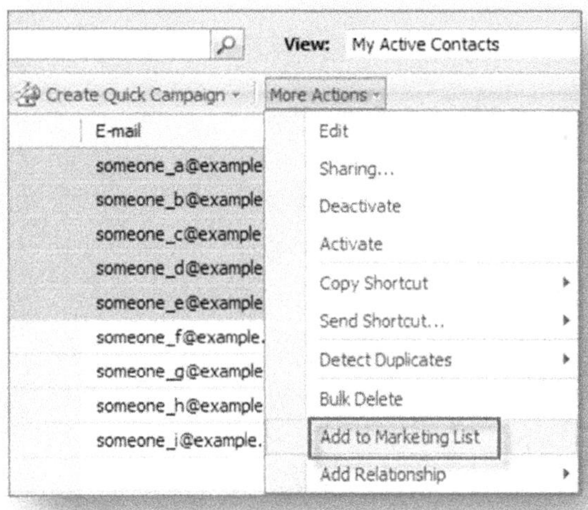

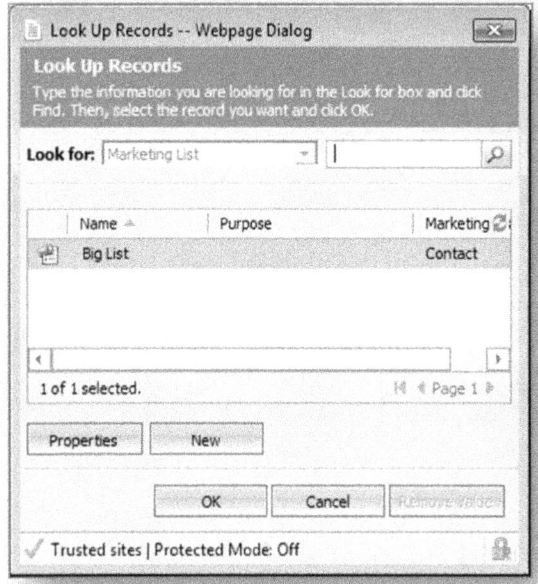

A marketing list without records is about as useful as an empty paper bag. Adding records to a marketing list is really easy, so you'll soon have lots of people and companies in your marketing lists.

It may be easiest to add records from a list view. This way, you can just highlight a few contacts, accounts, or leads - and then you're only two clicks away from dumping them into a marketing list.

Step-by-Step Instructions

1. In a list view, highlight a group of records.
2. Click the More Actions button on the Actions toolbar, and then click Add to marketing list.
3. Select a marketing list and click OK.

Tips & Tricks

- Use CTRL + CLICK in any list view to highlight multiple non-consecutive records.
- Use SHIFT + CLICK in any list view to highlight multiple consecutive records.
- To see more records on a list view by default, click Tools | Options (CRM | Options in Outlook) and then increase the maximum number of records shown per page.

Using lookup or Advanced Find to add members

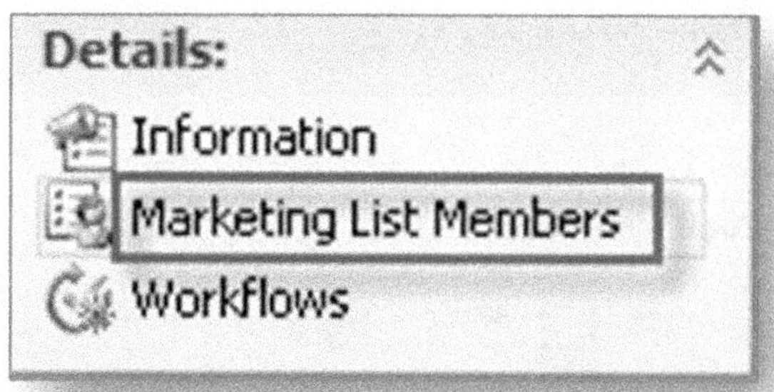

Advanced Find or Lookup can also be used to add members to a marketing list. This is really useful if you want a specific type of record to be added to your marketing list.

It can also be useful if you need to add more than just a few records to a marketing list. For example, if you need to add all 2,000 contacts in Montana to a marketing list, you'd want to use Advanced Find to add these people to your list.

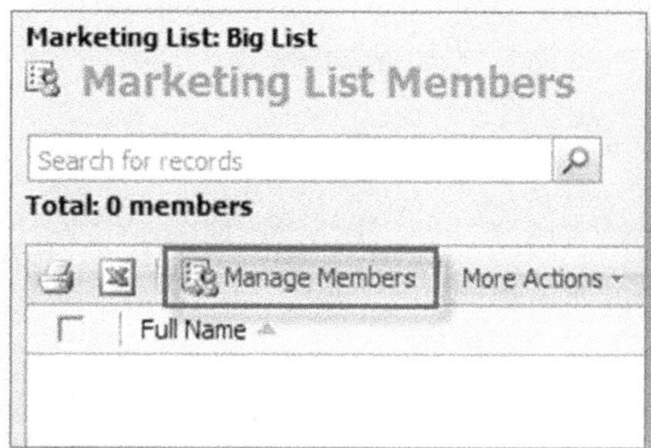

Step-by-Step Instructions

1. Open a marketing list.
2. Click Marketing List Members on the left.
3. Click Manage Members on the Actions toolbar.
4. Select either lookup or Advanced Find. Click OK.
5. You will be able to perform a lookup of records that will be pulled into the marketing list.

Tips & Tricks

- There is no easy way to undo the addition of records to a marketing list.

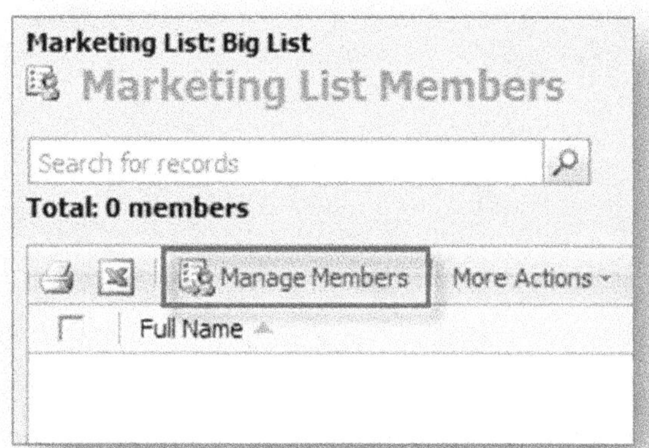

Using Advanced Find to remove or evaluate members

Do you have a record in your marketing list that isn't even worth dealing with? You can remove any record like this from your marketing list.

Let's say you want to remove all contacts in Montana from a marketing list. Using this procedure makes the mass removal simple.

Step-by-Step Instructions

1. Open a marketing list.
2. Click Marketing List Members on the left.
3. Click the Manage Members button on the Actions toolbar.
4. Choose to run an Advanced Find.
5. Highlight the contacts from the resulting Advanced Find Results screen that you want to remove and click the Remove from Marketing List button.

Tips & Tricks

- Again, there's no way to undo this action. So make sure you want to remove these records from a list before you start.

Modifying the list membership view

When you open a marketing list and look at the list of contacts, accounts or leads that are currently in the list, you can export this list easily to Excel. That's the good news.

The bad news is that it's not as easy to modify the columns in this view. If you need to add e-mail address, for example, you'll have to follow this procedure.

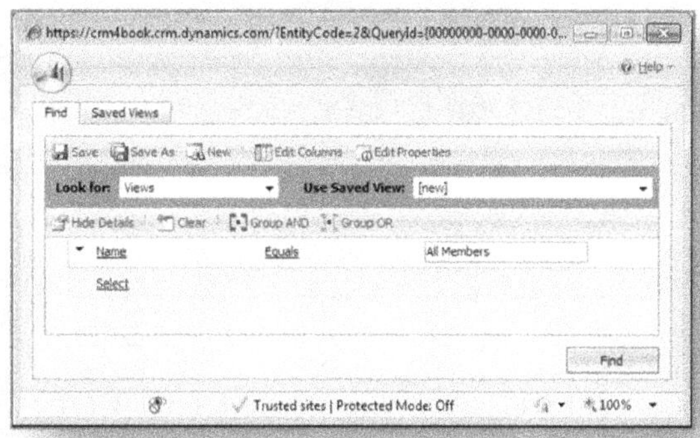

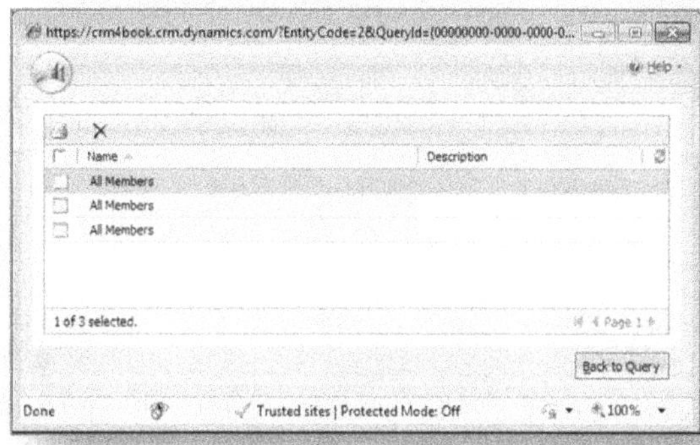

Step-by-Step Instructions

1. Click the Advanced Find button.
2. In the Look for drop-down, choose Views.
3. Configure your query to search for all views where the Name field equals All Members.
4. Double-click one of the three views that appears. One is for leads, the other is for contacts, and the last one is for accounts. You will have to figure out which is which.
5. Click the Add Columns button to add additional columns to the view.

Tips & Tricks

- You *must* publish customizations before any view changes will appear. To publish, go to Settings | Customization | Customize Entities. Then, from the More Actions drop-down, choose Publish All Customizations.

Viewing the marketing list information for a single record

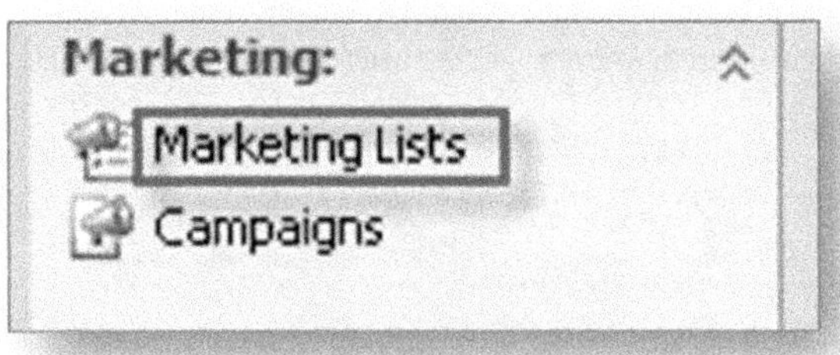

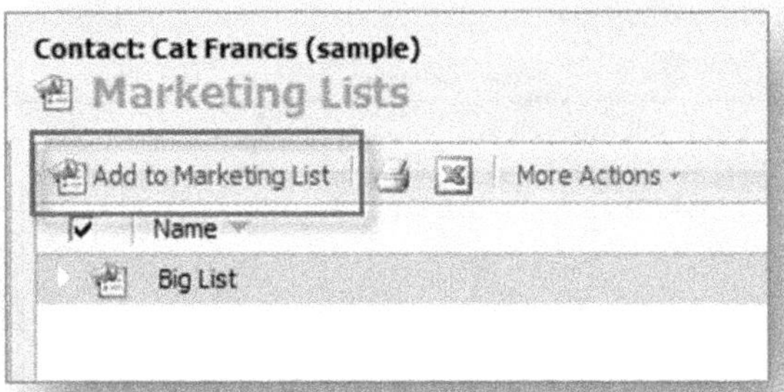

Do you want to check whether or not a record has been added to a marketing list? Want to keep track of which marketing lists a certain record belongs to. Fortunately, marketing lists for a single record can be easily viewed when you open a contact, account, or lead.

Step-by-Step Instructions

1. Open a record. (Either a contact, account, or lead record.)
2. On the left, click Marketing Lists.
3. A list of marketing lists that the current record belongs to will appear.

Tips & Tricks

➢ When viewing list membership for a contact, account, or lead record, you can click the Add to Marketing List button.

CHAPTER

14

Giving the appearance of a personalized touch with mail merge

Running a mail merge with Word ◆ Printing labels for records ◆ Saving your mail merge template mas an organization or personal template ◆ Recording a history of letters sent on individual records

Running a mail merge with Word

Mail merge in Microsoft Word is a great tool that can help your organization give a personalized touch. Because let's face it: In a business context, giving the perception of a personalized touch is more valuable than actually sitting down and touching each mail piece personally.

Mail merge in Microsoft CRM is best done using Microsoft Office Word, so you won't have to change your existing business process.

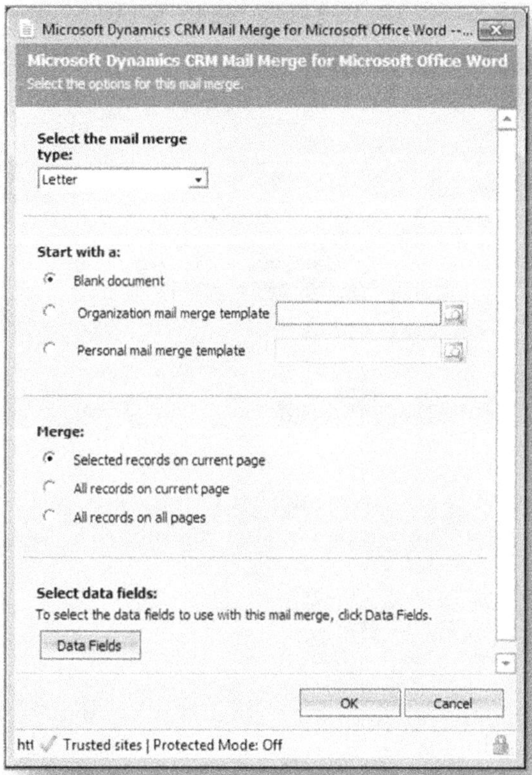

Step-by-Step Instructions

1. Highlight any records that you want to be included in your mail merge.
2. Click the Microsoft Word button on the toolbar.
3. Select a mail merge type, a template, and a merge range of records.
4. Click OK. A Word document will open directly to the Word mail merge wizard.
5. Complete the wizard to run your mail merge.

Tips & Tricks

- At the end of the mail merge, the system will prompt you to upload your template into the CRM system. This is a good idea if you will run a similar letter in the future.

Printing labels for records

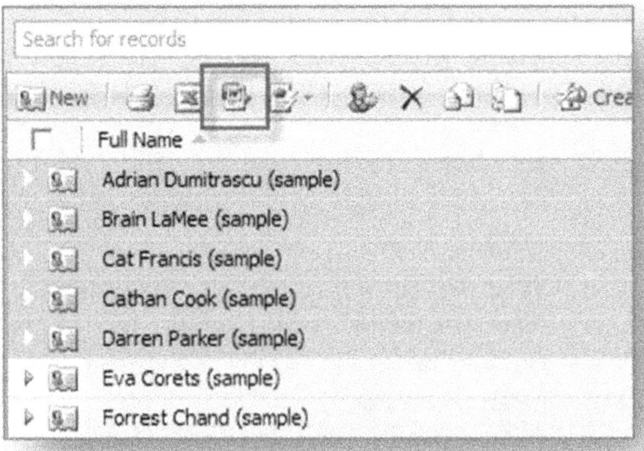

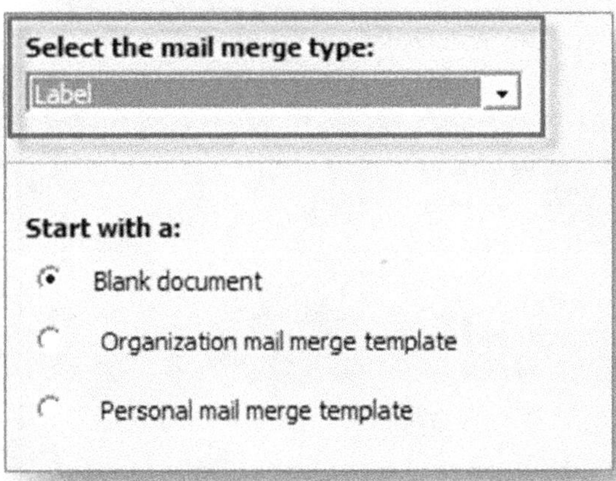

You don't actually print out labels by hand, do you? If you do, then you're a couple of decades behind the times and should be using mail merge to create labels for your records.

Printing labels is best done in Word, just like most of the other mail merges that you will do. Word is compatible with most sheet-fed label types, including Avery Labels.

Step-by-Step Instructions

1. Highlight a list of records. (Or go to a view that contains your records. Or perform an Advanced Find of the records for whom you'd like to print labels.)

2. Click the Word button on the toolbar. Select Labels from the drop-down.

3. Either select to use an existing template or create a mail merge from a blank document.

4. Click OK. A Word document will open, and it will open directly to the Word mail merge wizard.

Tips & Tricks

- Before printing your labels, it's a good idea to scan through them to make sure that all of the formatting (especially with foreign addresses) is correct.

Saving your mail merge template as an organization or a personal template

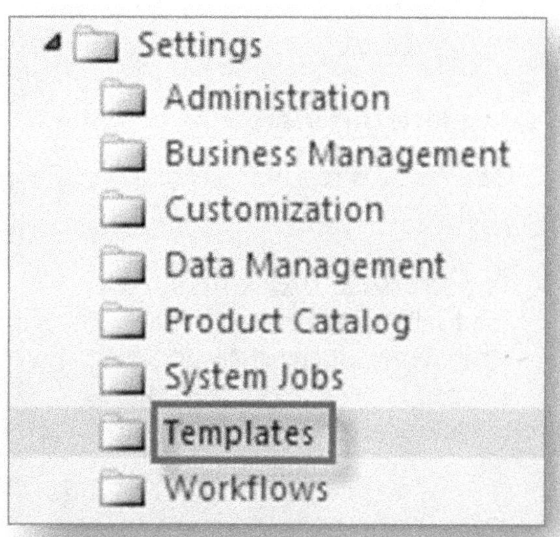

In Microsoft Dynamics CRM, you can save a mail merge template either as a personal template or an organizational template. The difference between the two has to do with ownership: personal templates are only available to you, while organizational documents are available to everyone.

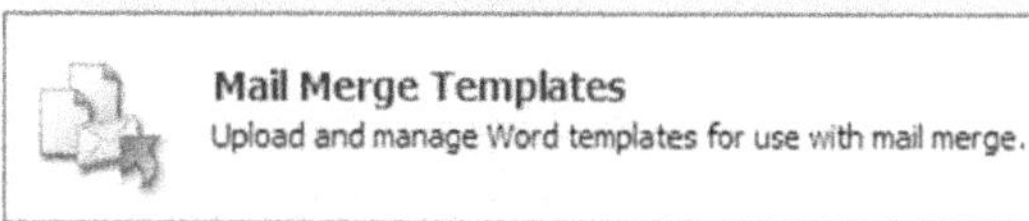

Note: At the end of running a mail merge, you'll have the option to upload the template to CRM. That may be easier than the instructions on this page.

Step-by-Step Instructions

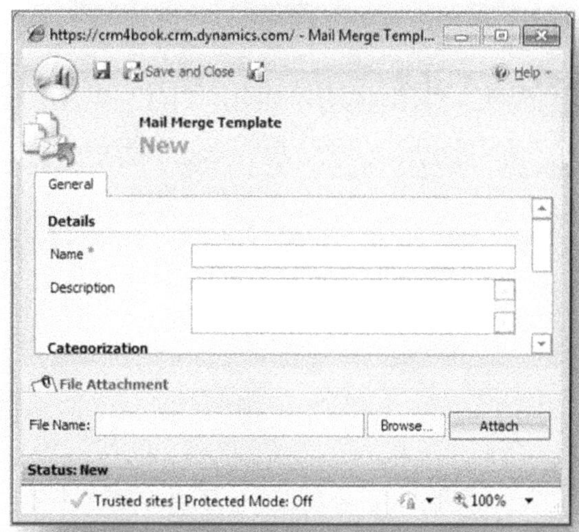

1. Click Settings on the Navigation Pane, and then click Templates.
2. Click the New button on the Actions toolbar.
3. Enter in important information about your template. Then click browse and locate the XML template file that you want to use.
4. Click Attach. This template will be saved as a personal template.
5. Click Settings on the Navigation Pane, and then click Templates.
6. Highlight the template. Click More Actions, then Make Available to Organization.

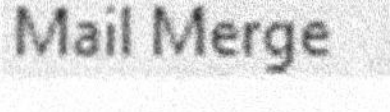

Complete the merge

Mail Merge is ready to produce your letters.

To personalize your letters, click "Edit Individual Letters." This will open a new document with your merged letters. To make changes to all the letters, switch back to the original document.

Merge

 Print...

 Edit individual letters...

 Upload Template to CRM

Step 4 of 4

 Previous: Preview your letters

Recording a history of letters sent to individual records

It's important to keep a history of all of the mail merges that you run. Otherwise you might send the same one multiple times, and that wouldn't look very professional.

When you print a mail merge, you are given the option to create a history of the merge.

Step-by-Step Instructions

1. Follow the mail merge process.
2. When you print the final merged document, you will be prompted to create a history.

Tips & Tricks

➢ If you forget to create a history, print the document again to XPS or PDF, and you'll get the prompt to create a history of the sent

CHAPTER 15

Too lazy to create a proper campaign? Try Quick Campaigns.

Scheduling a call with multiple records ◆ Running a Quick Campaign for marketing list members ◆ Viewing Quick Campaigns after they have been initiated

Scheduling a call with multiple records (Quick Campaigns)

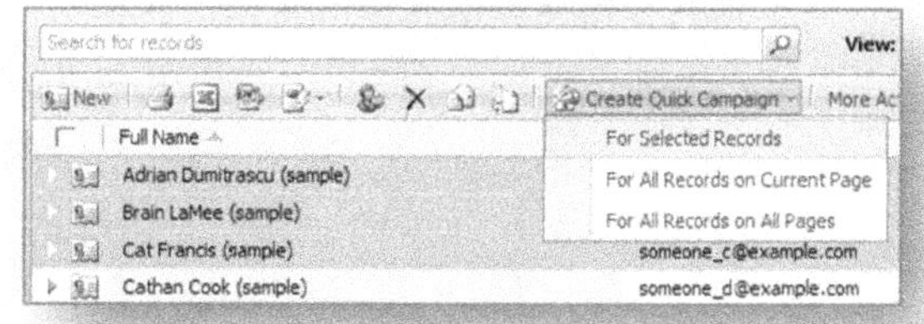

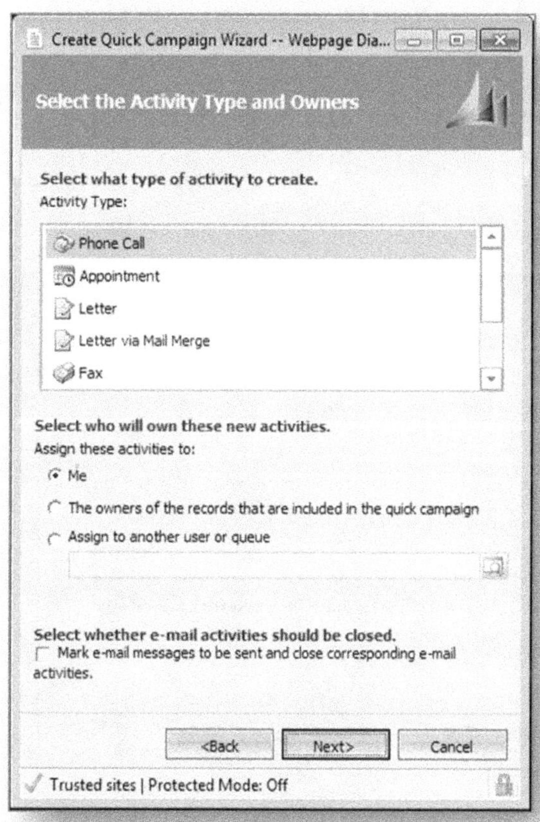

Are you having trouble keeping track of all of those different customers that you should be calling? Is your workstation overwhelmed with white sticky notes with phone numbers and times written on them? Should you call everyone from the trade show last week?

Microsoft Dynamics CRM allows you to schedule a call with multiple records. Phone calls scheduled in CRM will appear in Outlook as tasks.

Step-by-Step Instructions

1. Highlight a group of records, like contacts, leads, or accounts.
2. Click the Create Quick Campaign button on the toolbar. Choose the For Selected Records option from the drop-down.
3. Give your quick campaign a name and click Next.
4. Select Phone Call and click Next.
5. Specify content of the activity and click next.
6. Click Create. A phone call for each highlighted record will be created, and this record will sync with Outlook.

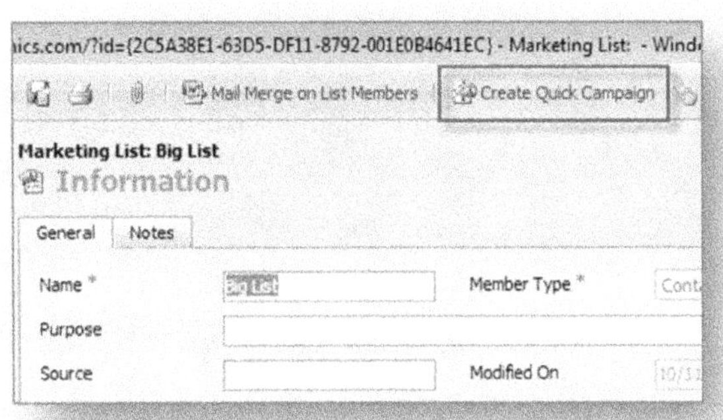

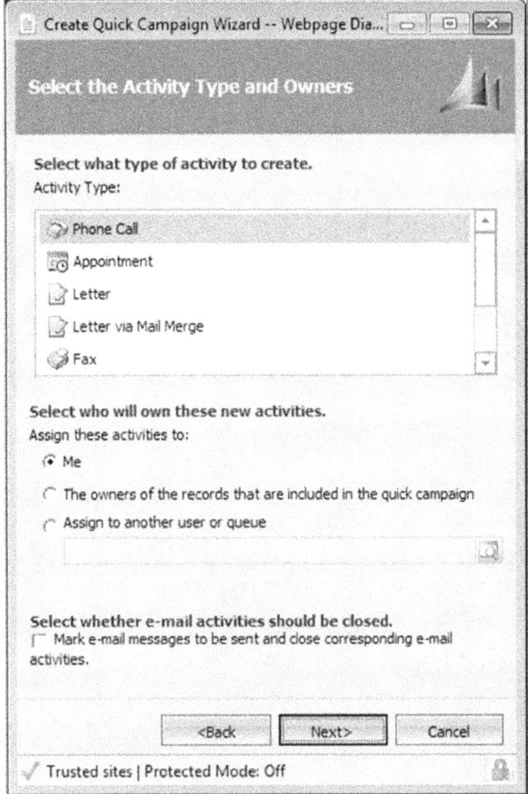

Running a Quick Campaign for marketing list members

Quick Campaigns are kind of like Campaigns, but they only have one campaign activity.

Running a Quick Campaign for bunch of marketing list members is a lot more efficient than going through your entire database and individually selecting records to add to your quick campaign.

Step-by-Step Instructions

1. Click Marketing in the Navigation Pane, and then click Marketing Lists.
2. Double-click a marketing list.
3. Click the Create Quick Campaign button on the toolbar and click Next.
4. Give your Quick Campaign a name and click Next.
5. Select the type of activity you'd like to create for your quick campaign and choose who will own these activities.
6. Add specific information for the type of activity that will be created and click Next. This activity (either a task, e-mail, letter, etc.) will be created for each marketing list member.

Viewing Quick Campaigns after they have been initiated

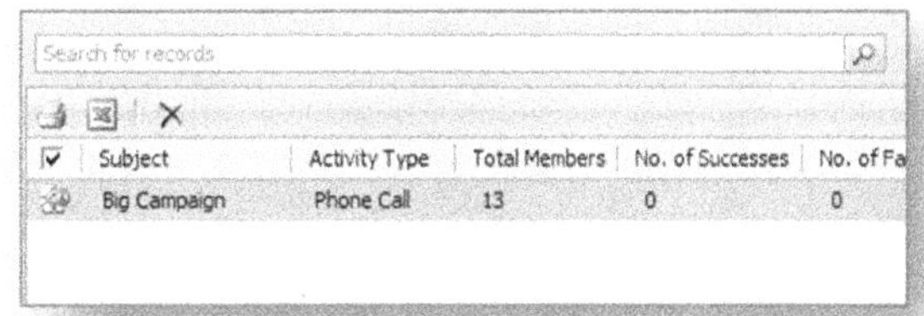

Need to check up on that Quick Campaign after it has been created? Not quite sure whether your configured it correctly?

Fortunately, Quick Campaigns can be easily viewed after they have been initiated.

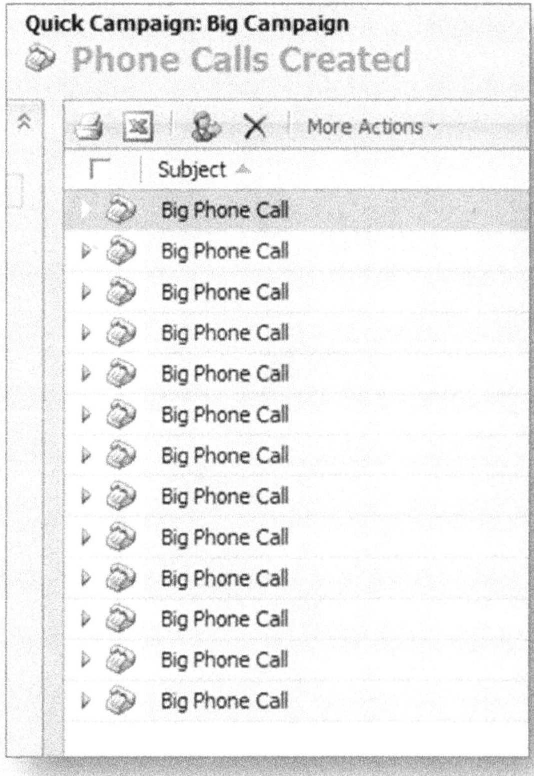

Step-by-Step Instructions

1. Click Marketing on the Navigation Pane, and then click Quick Campaigns.

2. Double-click a Quick Campaign. Here, you can see activities created from the quick campaign, campaign responses, a list of recipients for the campaign, and more.

Tips & Tricks

- If you have a complex campaign in the works that involves multiple e-mails, letters, or other marketing activities, consider creating a full campaign instead of a quick campaign.

CHAPTER

16

Managing Marketing Mayhem with Campaigns

Creating a campaign or campaign template ◆ Adding marketing lists to a campaign ◆ Adding planning tasks to a campaign ◆ Adding campaign activities ◆ Adding campaign responses

Creating a campaign or campaign template

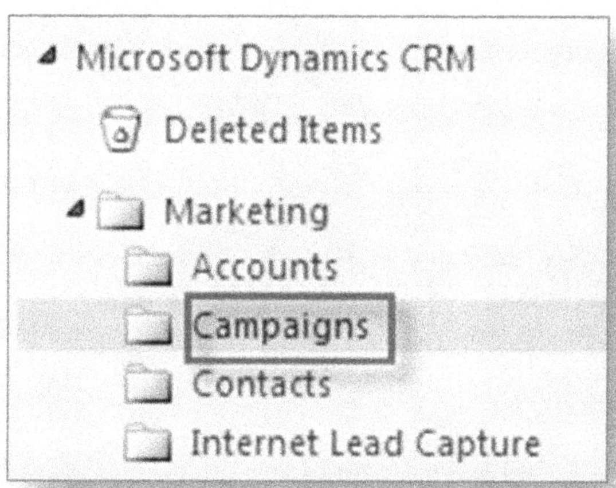

Campaigns are central to the marketing process. They allow you to organize a bunch of marketing activities together under a single campaign.

In Microsoft Dynamics CRM, you can either create a campaign or a campaign template. A campaign template will allow you to save and reuse a particular campaign's structure and apply it to other campaigns.

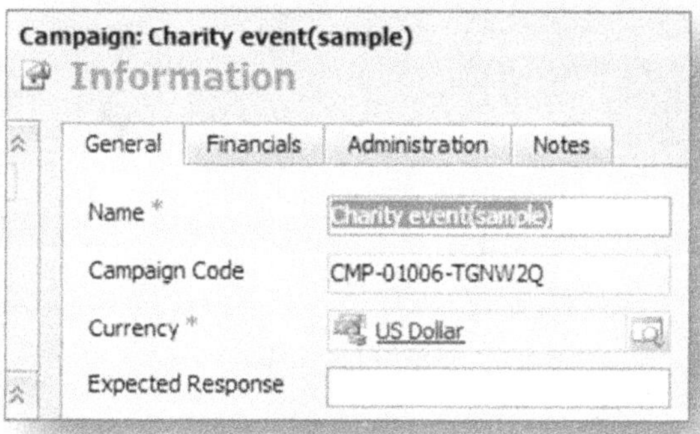

Step-by-Step Instructions

1. Click Marketing on the Navigation Pane, and then click Campaigns.
2. Click the New template button on the Actions toolbar.
3. Enter in a name for the campaign template.
4. Add planning tasks and marketing activities to the template.
5. Click Save and Close.

Tips & Tricks

- An example of where you'd use a campaign template: Let's say that four times a year, you do a customer renewal campaign. Create this campaign as a template, and then your planning tasks and marketing are easily replicated into each new campaign.

Adding marketing lists to a campaign

A campaign that targets a specific group of records would be much more successful than a campaign that targets an entire database.

Adding a marketing list to a campaign will give you a high level of control over who is targeted by your campaign. If you're targeting more than one type of record (like, for example, if you're targeting both current contacts and leads) then you'll need to have multiple marketing lists associated with your campaign.

Step-by-Step Instructions

1. Open a marketing campaign.
2. On the left, click Target Marketing Lists.
3. Click the Add button on the toolbar.
4. Check any marketing lists that you want to include in the campaign. Click OK.

Tips & Tricks

- A holiday mailer is a good example of a campaign that could have multiple marketing lists. You might have one list for people who should get a card an another list for people who should get a present.

Adding planning tasks to a campaign

Careful planning is the key to the success of a campaign. If you are planning a substantial campaign, such as a charity event, you will need some kind of resource that helps you to keep track of the internal tasks that you and your organization need to complete.

Adding planning tasks in Microsoft Dynamics CRM will help you manage various internal tasks, and it will also help you evaluate whether the effort to launch the campaign was worth the monetary result.

Step-by-Step Instructions

1. Open a Campaign.
2. On the left, click Planning Tasks.
3. Click New.
4. Fill in information about your planning task and click save and close.
5. Repeat this process until all planning tasks are in the system.

Tips & Tricks

- Examples of planning tasks include: buying stamps, licking envelopes, printing labels, designing postcards, getting executive approval for artwork and text copy, internal meetings to cover strategy, etc.

Adding campaign activities

Campaign activities are the bulk of your campaign. Any activity, like a phone call or e-mail, can be added to a campaign in Microsoft Dynamics CRM. You can even add a mail merge to as a campaign activity.

Campaign activities are the activities that involve some level of direct interaction with your customer.

Step-by-Step Instructions

1. Open a Campaign.
2. On the left, click Campaign Activities.
3. Click the New button on the Actions toolbar.
4. Enter information about the activity. Click Save and Close.
5. Repeat this process until all campaign activities are entered into your system.

Tips & Tricks

- Examples of campaign activities include: Sending a postcard, sending an e-mail blast, engaging a telemarketing effort, sending out a survey, inviting people to an event, and so on.

Adding campaign responses

Do you want to know if all of your hard work on a marketing campaign has paid off? Campaign responses help you determine how effective a particular campaign is.

Adding campaign responses manually is pretty painful. Most people set up systems to automate the creation of these campaign responses, either through third-party add-on products or through the built-in Workflow feature.

Step-by-Step Instructions

1. Open a campaign.
2. On the left, click Campaign Responses.
3. Click the New button on the Actions toolbar.
4. Enter in any important information about your campaign response.
5. Click Save and Close.

Tips & Tricks

- If you integrate a third party e-mail system like CoreMotives or ExactTarget, then each read/open/click on an outgoing e-mail will be recorded in the system as a campaign response.

CHAPTER

17

Let's make some money on the web with Internet Lead Capture

Configuring Internet Lead Capture ◆ Creating a landing page ◆ Capturing and assigning leads entered on your web form

Configuring Internet Lead Capture

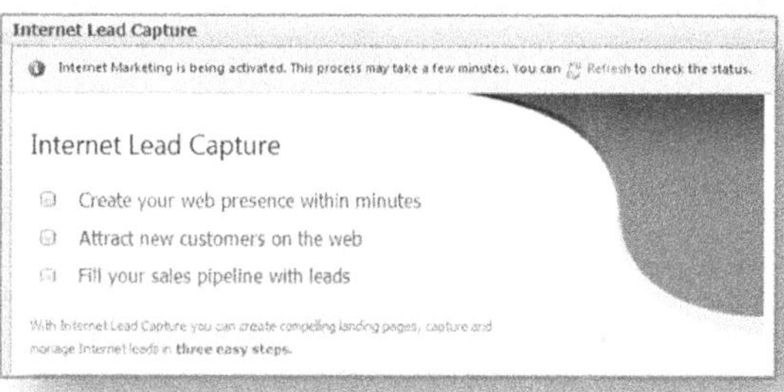

Just about everyone has a form on their company web site that allows a user to enter information that gets transmitted to someone in the organization.

You can use the Internet Lead Capture feature in CRM to pull data from these web forms directly into your database.

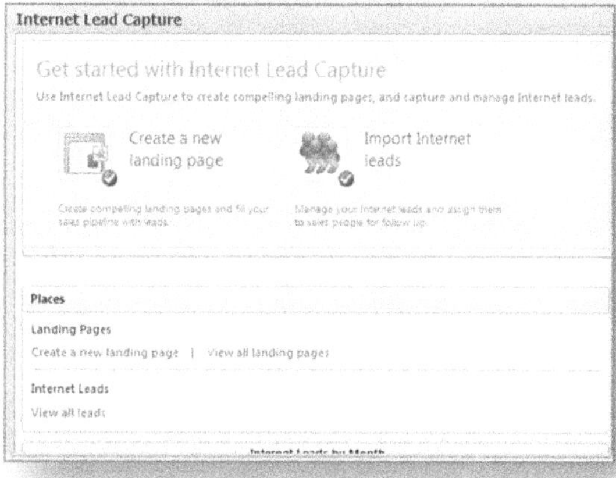

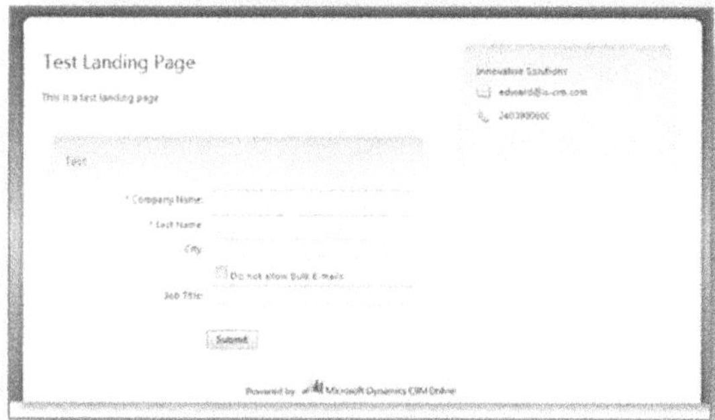

Step-by-Step Instructions

1. On the Navigation Pane, click Sales and then Internet Lead Capture.

2. Click Get Started.

3. You will see an option at the top of the screen to refresh when your account has been configured for Internet Lead Capture. Wait a few minutes and click it.

4. You're now ready to create landing pages and start using the Internet Lead Capture feature.

Tips & Tricks

- Some security roles will not have sufficient rights to configure or use the internet marketing features in CRM.

- Once you have configured your database for Internet Lead Capture, you won't have to run through these steps again.

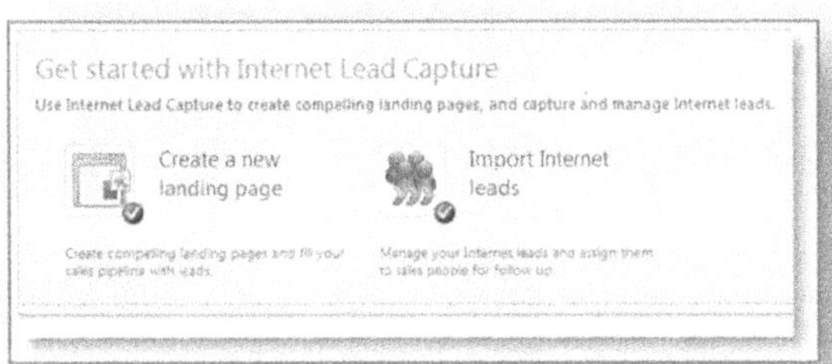

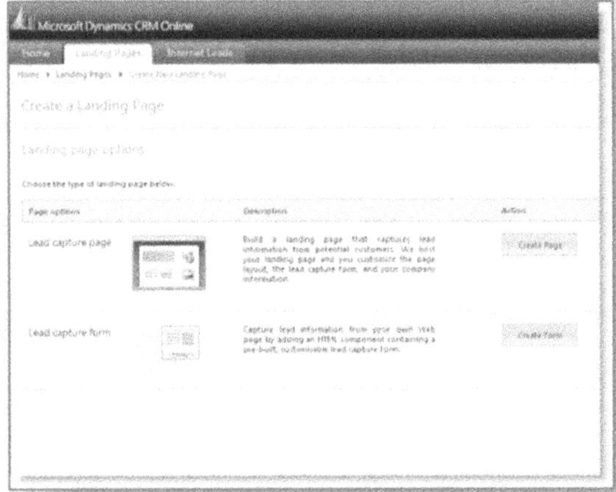

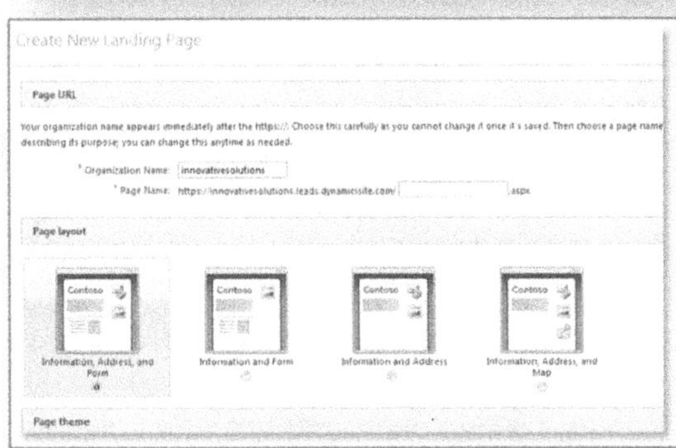

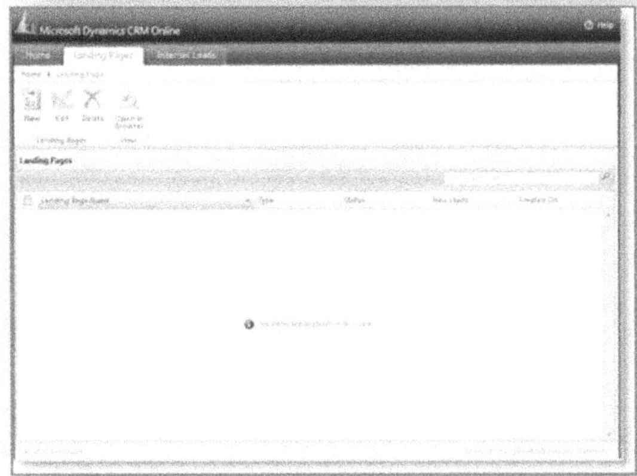

Create a landing page

Landing pages are the web pages where your prospects could fill out a form and have their information delivered directly to your CRM database.

Landing pages can be hosted on the Microsoft site (for free), or the system can give you the HTML code required to incorporate landing pages into your existing web site infrastructure.

Step-by-Step Instructions

1. On the Navigation Pane, click Sales and then Internet Lead Capture.

2. Click the Create a New Landing Page option.

3. Click the Create Page button if you'd like Microsoft to host the landing page.

4. Click the Create Form button if you'd like to create HTML form code to incorporate into your web site.

5. Follow the on-screen instructions to create your HTML form coede or hosted landing page. You'll need to specify the fields from CRM that you want to incorporate into the form.

Capturing and assigning leads entered on your web form

When a potential customer visits your web site and enters information into your Internet Lead Capture form, that information automatically transfers into CRM.

Records don't transfer directly into your live database. Rather, they show up in a temporary holding area, where someone on your marketing staff will likely be responsible for either approving/deleting the submissions.

Step-by-Step Instructions

1. On the Navigation Pane, click Sales and then Internet Lead Capture.
2. Click the Import Internet Leads option.
3. Highlight one or more leads and click either the Assign to Me or Assign to Others buttons.

Tips & Tricks

- If you assign leads to others, it might be a good idea to make sure that a workflow has been set up that will notify users by e-mail that a lead has been assigned to them.

CHAPTER 18

OK, so you have a screaming customer on the phone (Cases)

Creating a customer service case ◆ Assigning a knowledge base article to a case ◆ Adding case notes and activities ◆ Deleting or cancelling a case ◆ Resolving a case ◆ Managing service queues

Creating a customer service case

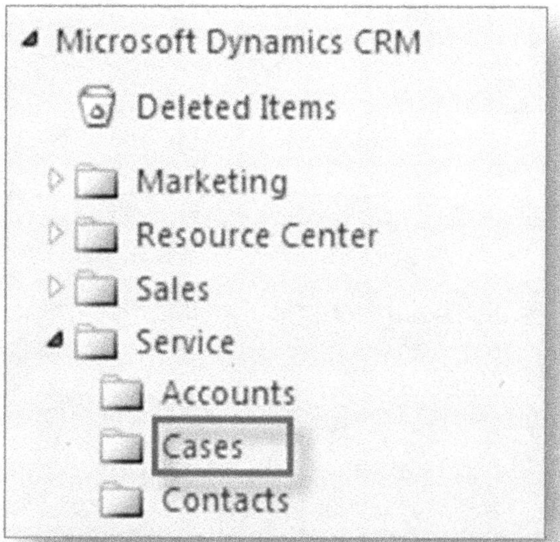

While we all sometimes wish we could ignore our customers after a sale has been made, businesses that thrive are usually those with strong post-sales customer service.

It's easy to create and manage your service cases in Microsoft Dynamics CRM. Managing incidents in CRM will help your service techs keep track of all of the work that they need to do.

Step-by-Step Instructions

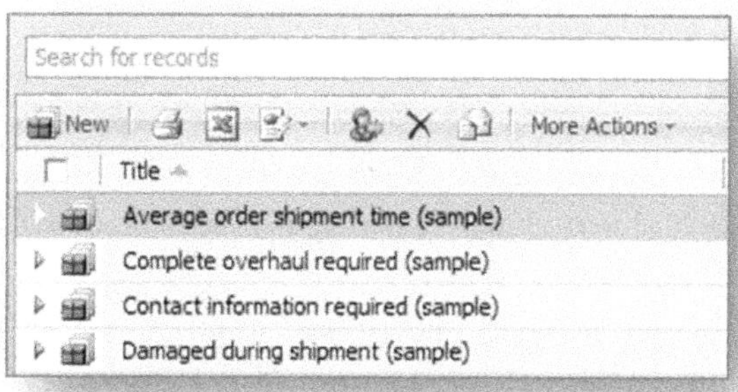

1. Click Service on the Navigation Pane, and then click Cases.
2. Click New on the Actions toolbar.
3. Enter in important information about your service case. Click Save and Close.

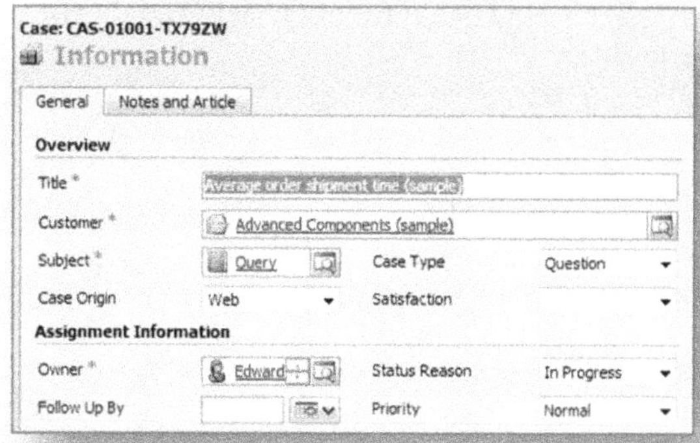

Tips & Tricks

- If you require that customers who call for service have an active contract in place, you can link these cases to contract and contract lines.
- Each contract line within a contract allows the customer to have either a certain number of incidents or a certain number of minutes.

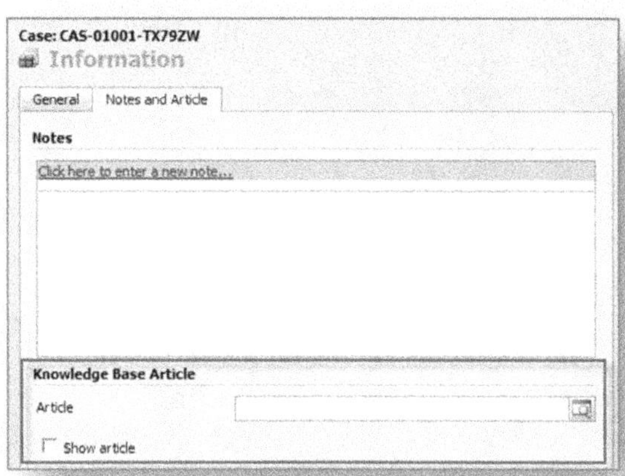

Assigning a knowledge base article to a case

Knowledge base articles help you keep track of all of the technical information that is needed for service requests.

Things like FAQs, how-tos, and bug-fixes are all examples of knowledge base articles. They can be assigned to a particular service case for quick reference.

Step-by-Step Instructions

1. Open a service case.
2. Click the Notes and Articles Tab.
3. Under Knowledge Base, click Lookup.
4. Search for your article.
5. Select the article and click OK.

Tips & Tricks

- Only one KB article can be linked to each service case in CRM. If more are required, you may just enter the KB numbers in the case notes.
- If the word "Case" doesn't fit your business, you could change the name of cases to Incidents, Complaints, or something more appropriate. This is done in Settings | Customize | Customize Entities.

Adding case notes and activities

Any time you create a case in the system, you'll need to add case notes (and sometimes activities) to complete the record of contact with the customer.

You've probably been on the phone with a phone company or big corporation where the support technician had to look at your notes to see what the last technician had done with your account?

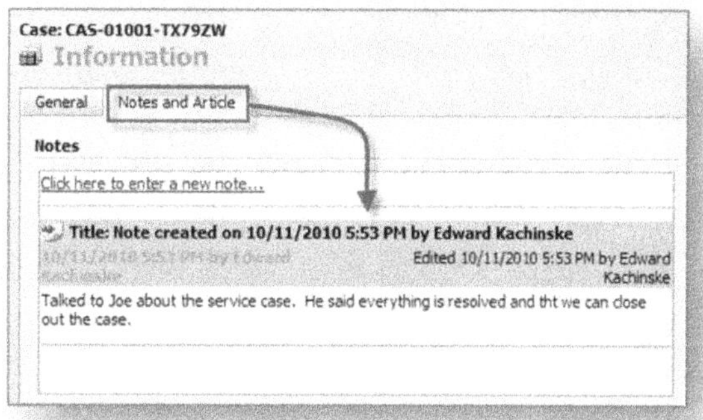

Step-by-Step Instructions

1. Open a service case.
2. Click the Notes and Articles tab.
3. Click in the space provided to add a new note for this case. When you are finished, click outside of the notes area to see that your name and the current date have been appended to the note.
3. Click the Follow-up button on the toolbar to add a follow-up task or appointment linked back to the case.

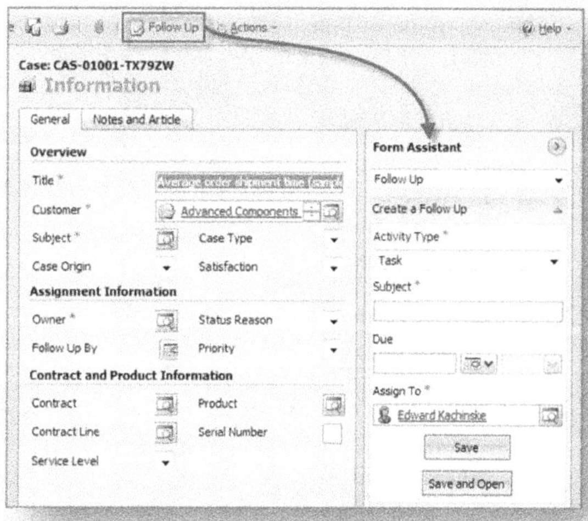

Tips & Tricks

- In Outlook, you can also link an appointment or task back to a specific task. Open the activity and click the Set Regarding button on the ribbon. In the record type drop-down, choose Cases.

Deleting or cancelling a case

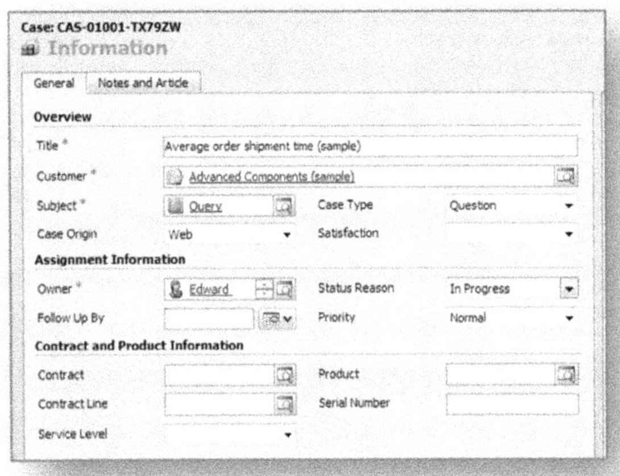

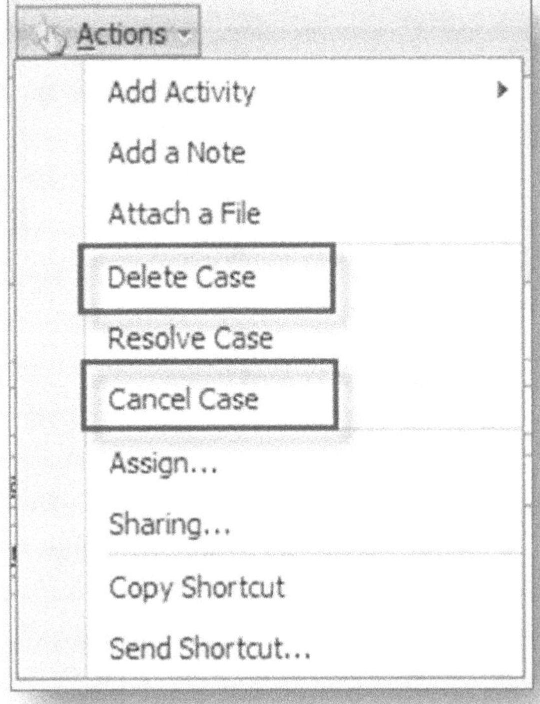

Did you accidentally enter a case into the system and then realize that no case was really needed? Then delete it out of the system, and you will never have to think about it again.

If a customer calls to cancel a customer service incident, you can also cancel it.

Step-by-Step Instructions

1. Open a service case.
2. Click the Actions button on the toolbar, then Delete or Cancel Case.

Tips & Tricks

- Deleting a case permanently removes it from the system. Once deleted, there is no option to undelete the record.
- Canceling a case sends the case into a canceled status.

Resolving a case

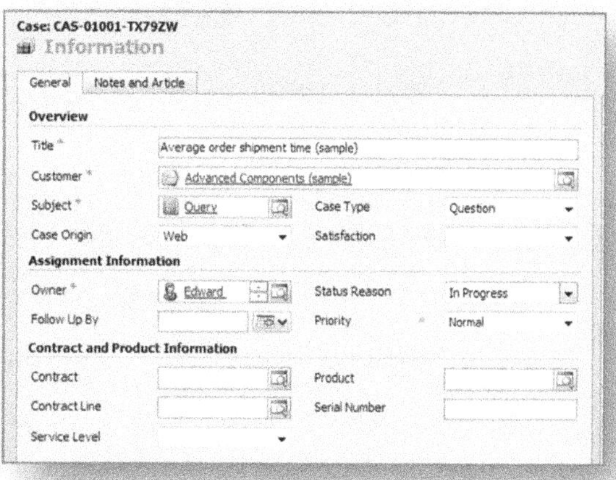

Eventually, you'll hit a point where you will successfully resolve a case.

If you have helped a customer successfully, then you will want to resolve the case ASAP. You wouldn't want other technicians working on one of your resolved cases, would you?

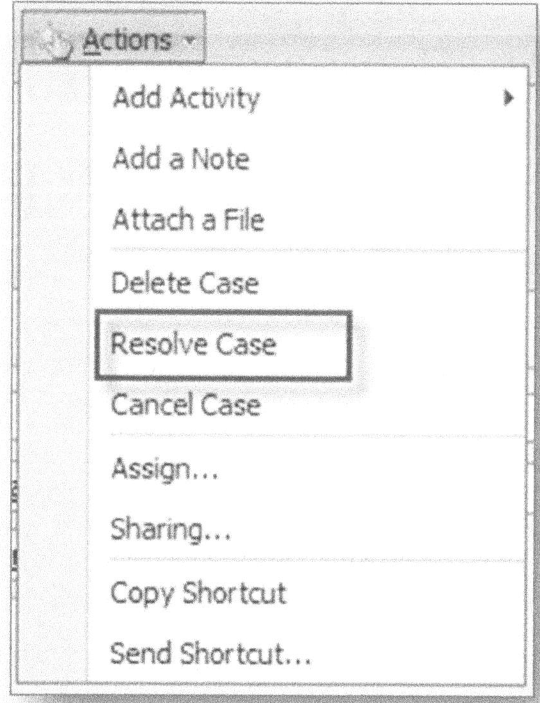

Step-by-Step Instructions

1. Open a case.
2. Click the Actions button, then Resolve Case.
3. Enter in any important information about your case and click OK.

Tips & Tricks

- If you resolve a case and then realize that the issue wasn't actually resolved, you can reactivate a resolved case. Just go to your list of resolved cases and open the case. From the Actions drop-down, you'll be able to reactivate the case.
- You should probably create workflow alongside the resolution of cases in CRM. So, when a customer service case is resolved, an e-mail could automatically go out to the end customer to let him/her know that the issue has been resolved.

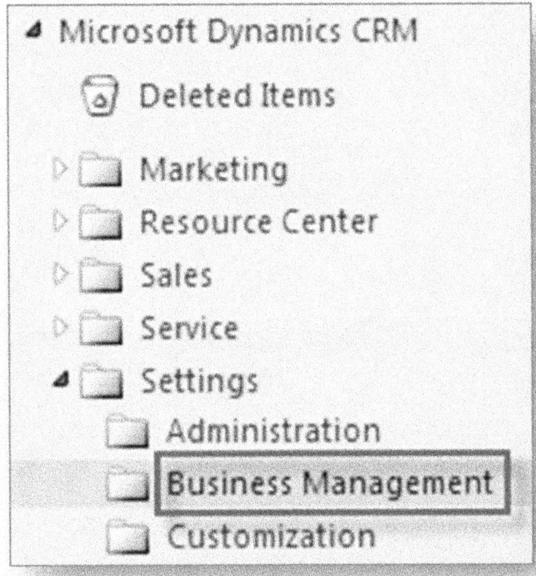

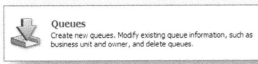

Queues
Create new queues. Modify existing queue information, such as business unit and owner, and delete queues.

Managing service queues

If you have more than one customer service representative, you'll probably want to have a queue to manage distribution of cases within your support department. Cases can be assigned to a queue, and then the next available rep can accept the cases that best fit their skill sets.

If you see a case in a service queue that you want to take on, accept it, and it will be assigned to you.

Step-by-Step Instructions

1. Click Settings on the Navigation Pane, and then click Business Management. (Or click the Workplace.)
2. Click Queues.
3. Click the New button to create a new queue.

Tips & Tricks

- Cases that you have accepted will appear in your In Progress queue.

CHAPTER

19

No shoes, no contract, no service.

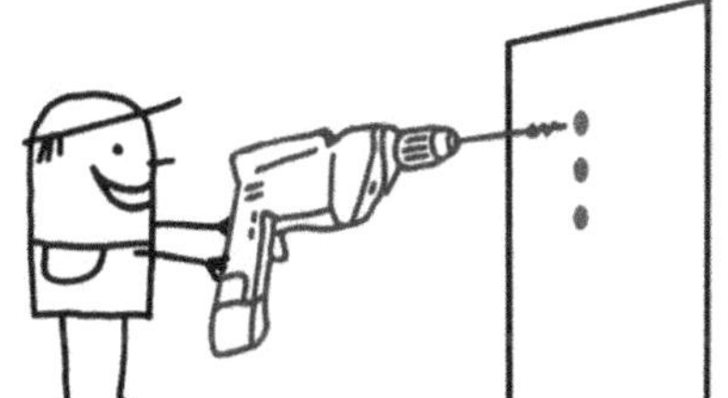

Creating a service contract template ◆ Creating a contract from a template ◆ Adding contract lines to a contract ◆ Linking service cases to a contract ◆ Invoicing a contract ◆ Copying/renewing a contract.

Creating a service contract template

Service contracts are important for your business because they help you manage the various service options that you offer your customers. They also enforce paid service engagements.

Before you begin creating service contracts, you need to create a contract template, which acts as a mold for your various service contracts.

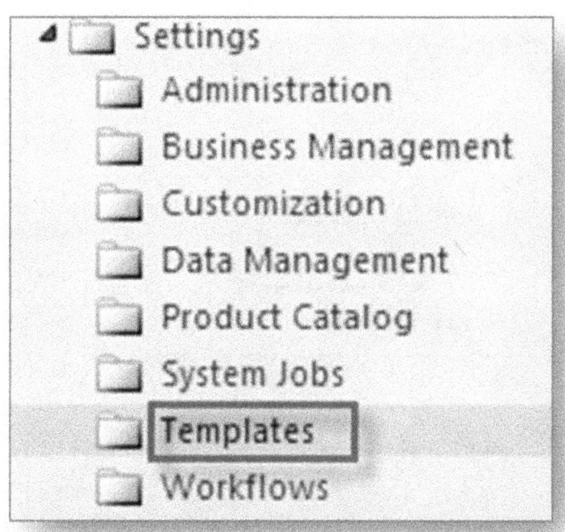

Step-by-Step Instructions

1. Click Settings on the Navigation Pane, and then click Templates.
2. Click Contract Templates.
3. Click the New button on the Taskbar.
4. Enter in information about your contract template, such as the name or the allotment type.
5. Click Save and Close.

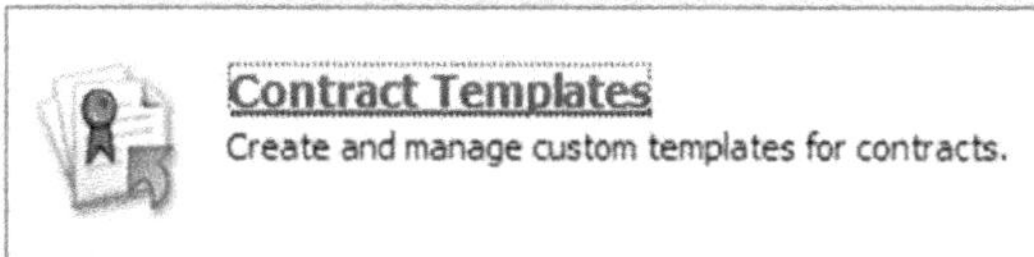

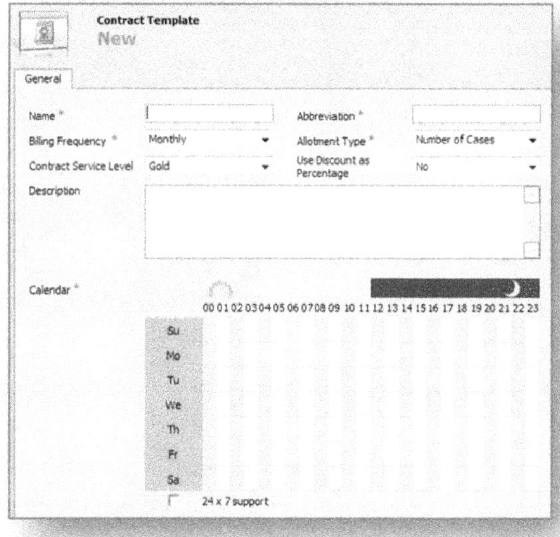

Tips & Tricks

- Service contacts can have two types of allotments: incidents or minutes. A support contract could offer a certain number of minutes as its deliverable, or it could offer a certain number of calls/incidents.

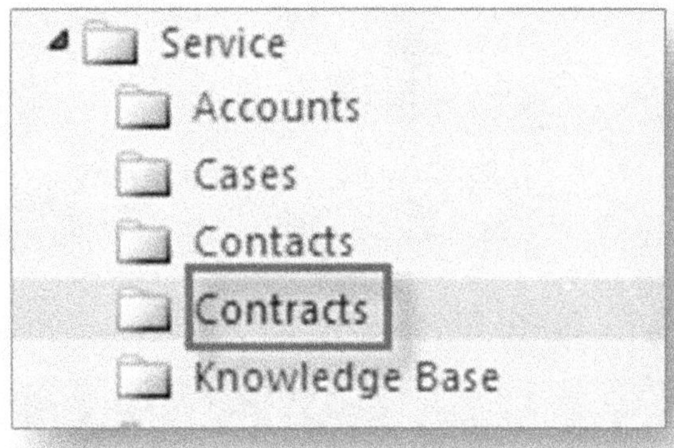

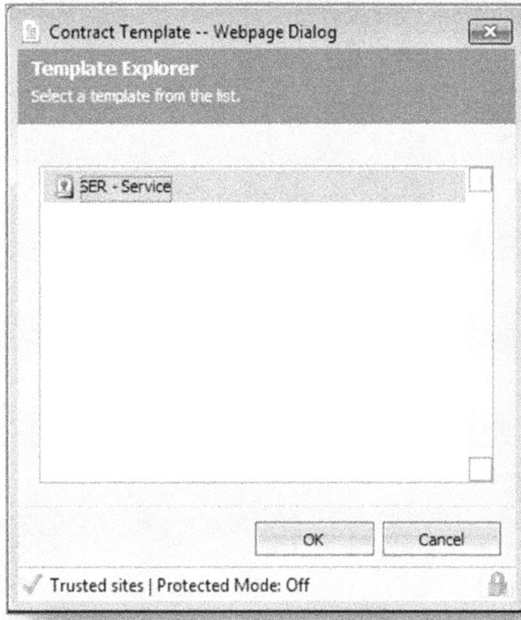

Creating a contract from a template

Have you created a contract template? Then you are ready to create an actual service contract from that template. This service contract will contain the service agreement between you an actual customer.

It's important to note that the contract itself does not actually offer any specific deliverables to your customer. That comes with contract lines, which are covered on the next page.

Step-by-Step Instructions

1. Click Service on the Navigation Pane, and then click Contracts.

2. Click the New button on the Actions toolbar.

3. Choose the template for your service contract.

4. Give your contract a name, customer, start/end date, bill-to name, and any other information.

5. Click the Save button.

Tips & Tricks

- You won't be able to link any cases to this service contract until the contract has been invoiced.

- This contract will only be valid between the start/end dates. Outside of these dates, the contract will be invalid.

Adding contract lines to a contract

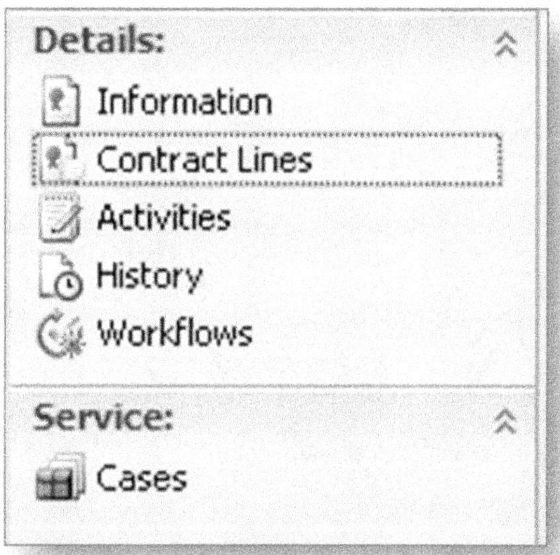

Once you have a contract set up, you need to add contract lines to add the details of the contract.

Think of contract lines as the individual deliverables that make up the service contract. If you were a plumber, for instance, you might have a contract line designating a certain number of service visits to an office building.

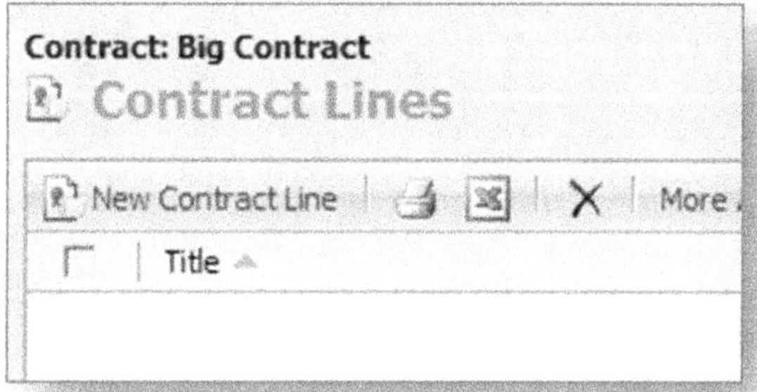

Step-by-Step Instructions

1. Open a contract.
2. On the left, click Contract Lines.
3. Click New Contract Line on the toolbar.
4. Enter in information about your contract line, like the total number of cases or minutes allowed under this contract line.
5. Click Save and Close.

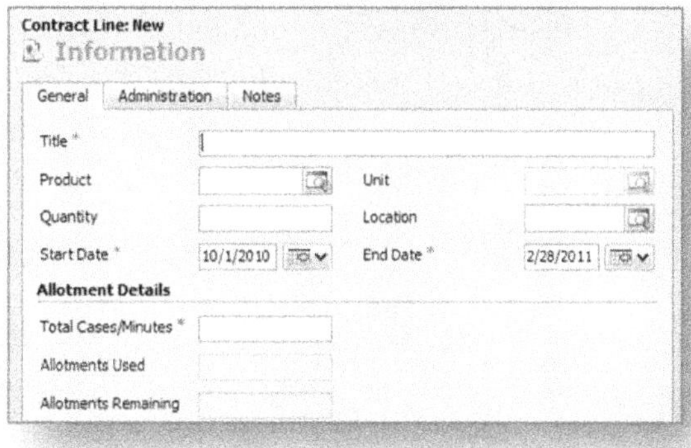

Tips & Tricks

- If your contract line allowed for 15 cases on a contract, then each time you link a case to this contract line, the number allotments will automatically reduce by 1 for each case entered into the system.
- The total price of the contract is calculated as the sum total price of the contract lines.

Linking service cases to a contract

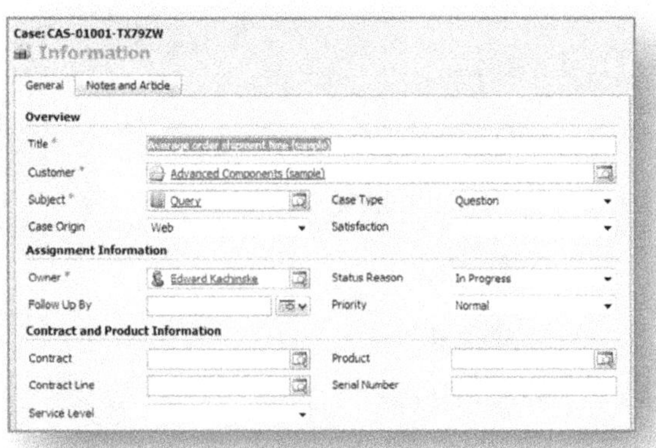

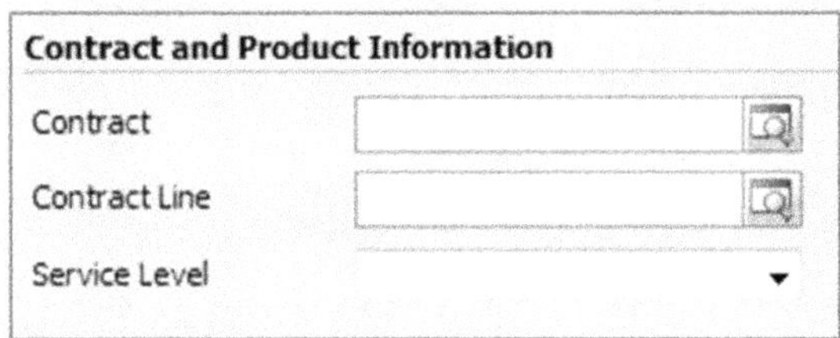

It is very important to link your service cases to a service contract if you are in the kind of business where you charge for support. If your company provides free support to customers, then you can likely skip over all of the stuff in this chapter related to contracts.

Linking cases and contract lines together will ensure that your customers get their correct service allotments. It also will ensure that you don't give out any free service.

Step-by-Step Instructions

1. Open a case.
2. Locate the Contract field. Click the lookup button to the right of this field and choose a contract.
3. Just under the Contract field, click the lookup button on the Contract Line field. This will bring up a list of contract lines on the contract (chosen in step 2). Choose a contract line.

Tips & Tricks

- The system will *only* display valid/current contracts. So, if a contract is expired or hasn't yet been invoiced, then you won't be able to link a case to it.

Invoicing a contract

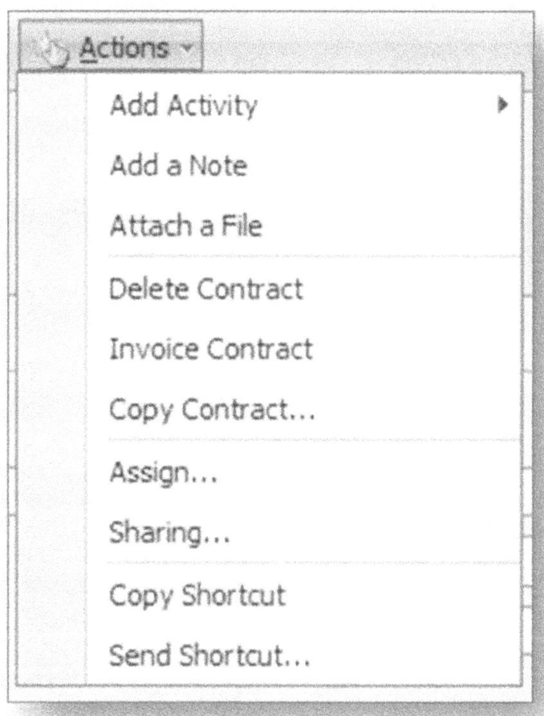

Once a contract is ready to activate, you should invoice it. Only invoiced contracts will show up in the system as current contract. Anything that hasn't been invoiced is just pending.

Once a contract has been invoiced, it cannot be edited or deleted. Contracts are only valid between the start and end dates after they have been invoiced.

Step-by-Step Instructions

1. Open a contract that has at least one contract line.
2. Click Actions on the toolbar, then Invoice Contract.

Tips & Tricks

- If you invoice a contract, it becomes read-only. There is no way to un-invoice a contract, so your only option if you need to change the terms of the contract would be to renew the contract and then delete the original contract.

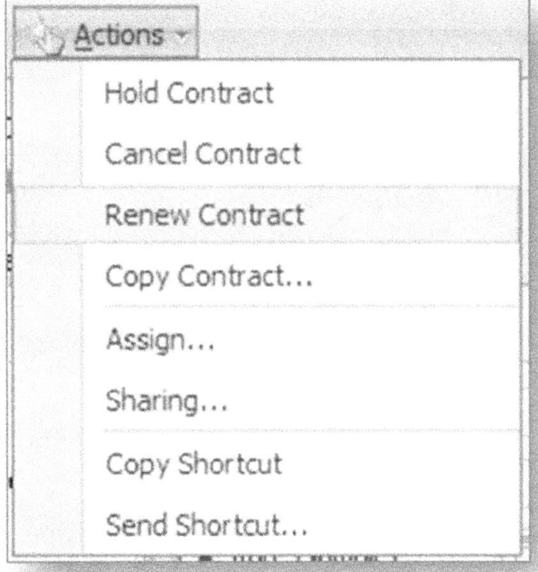

Copying/renewing a contract

Have you done such a good job servicing that your customer has decided to renew his or her service contract? Give yourself a pat on the back and renew the service contract in Microsoft Dynamic CRM.

Only active/invoiced contracts can be renewed, and renewing a contract can copy over all of the information from the original contract, including contract lines.

Step-by-Step Instructions

1. Open an active contract.
2. Click Actions on the toolbar, then Renew Contract.
3. Select whether you'd like to include canceled contract lines.
4. Click OK.

Tips & Tricks

- Only invoiced contracts can be renewed, but pre-invoiced contracts can be copied. Just open the contract and click Actions | Copy Contract.
- In the Settings | Administration | Auto-Numbering, you can modify the default format for the automatically generated contract numbers that are assigned to each contract.

Don't ask me – look it up in the KB.

Searching or browsing knowledge base articles ◆ Creating a new knowledge base template ◆ Creating a new knowledge base article from a template ◆ Submitting and approving knowledge base articles ◆ Adding comments to a knowledge base article

Searching or browsing knowledge base articles

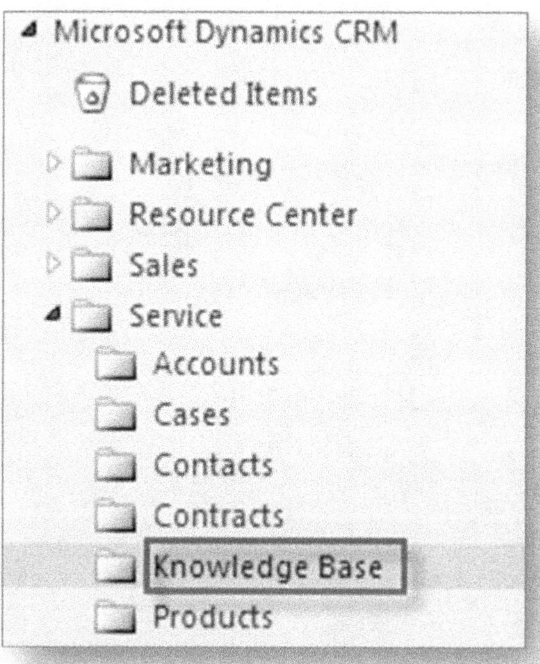

Do you know everything? Likely not. For those times when you don't know the customer's answer off the top of your head, CRM has a knowledge base - a searchable database of bug fixes, how-to's, and other great document.

The knowledge base is a fantastic resource that allows you to manage and use all of the documents that help you resolve service cases.

Step-by-Step Instructions

1. Click Service on the Navigation Pane, and then click Knowledge Base.

2. Click the drop-down in the top left of the screen and select Full Text Search.

3. Run your search.

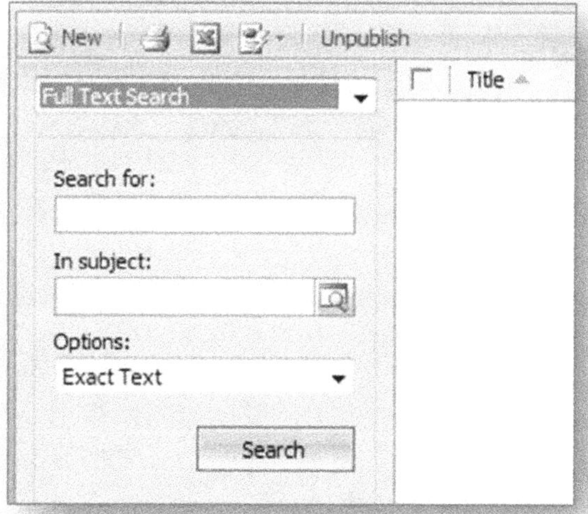

Tips & Tricks

- You can also browse knowledge base documents by subject. Instead of choosing the Full Text Search option on the drop down, select to browse by subject.

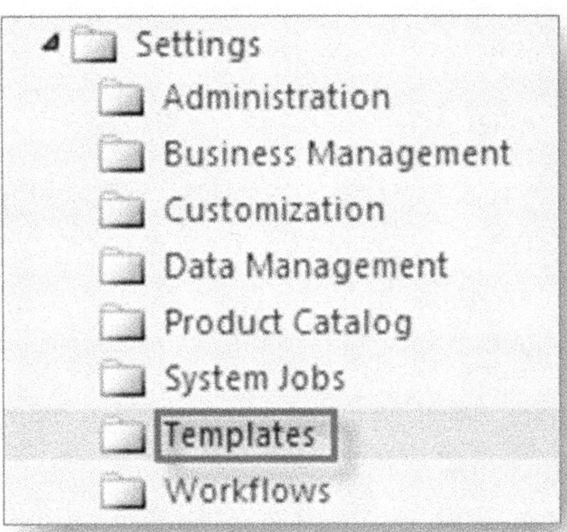

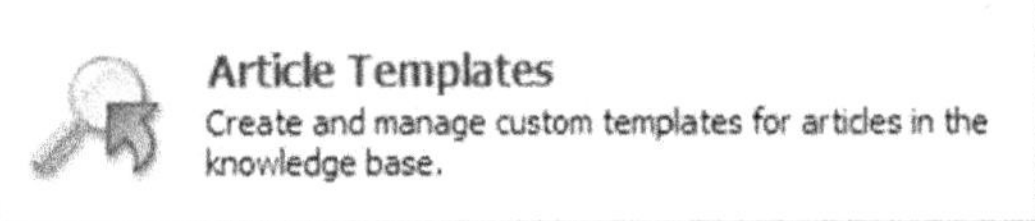

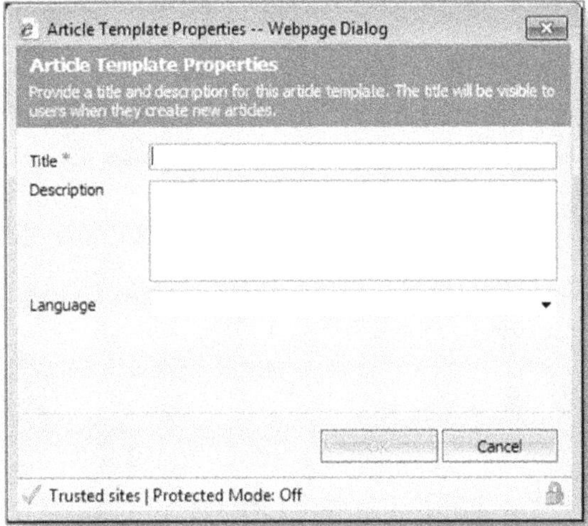

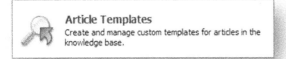

Creating a knowledge base template

Before you begin creating knowledge base articles, you need to create a knowledge base template. A knowledge base template is basically a framework on which subsequent knowledge base articles will be based.

The template contains the main sections that will appear in the actual documents. For example, you might create a template that includes a section to identify the question, another section to identify the answer, and a third section to identify additional resources.

Step-by-Step Instructions

1. Click Settings on the Navigation Pane, and then click Templates.
2. Click Article Templates.
3. Click the New button on the Actions toolbar.
4. Give your template a title and any sections that you want to the template.
5. Click Save and Close.

Tips & Tricks

- Basic knowledge base templates include a question section and an answer section. Add more sections to meet your business requirements.

Creating a new knowledge base article from a template

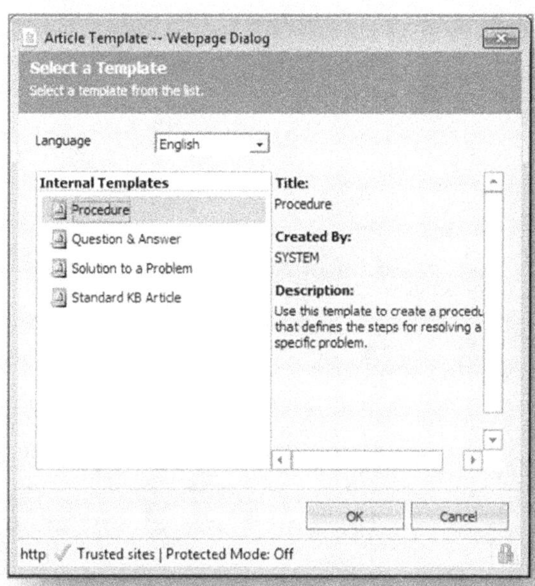

You want to make life easier for your fellow service technicians, right? Then create a knowledge base article after you have resolved a case.

Once the issue is in the knowledge base, other service technicians will be able to solve the same problem quickly and efficiently.

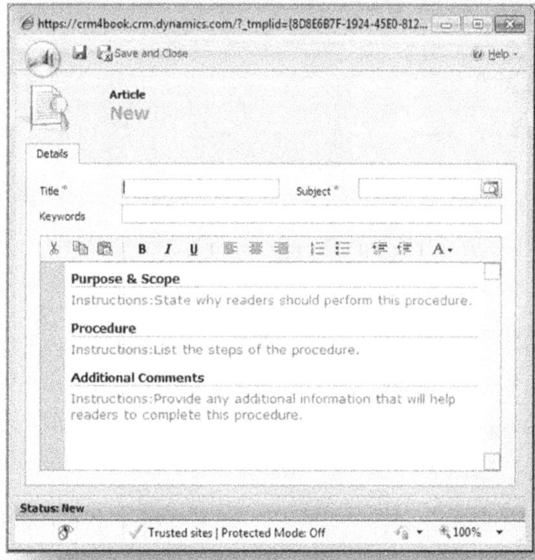

Step-by-Step Instructions

1. Click Service on the Navigation Pane, and then click Knowledge Base.
2. Click the New button on the Actions toolbar.
3. Select a template and click OK.
4. Fill out the knowledge base article and click Save and Close.

Tips & Tricks

- You can only create knowledge base documents from a template. There is no freeform ability to create a KB document.

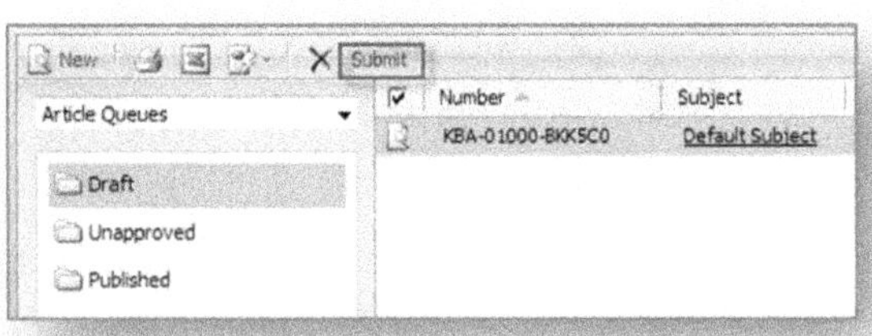

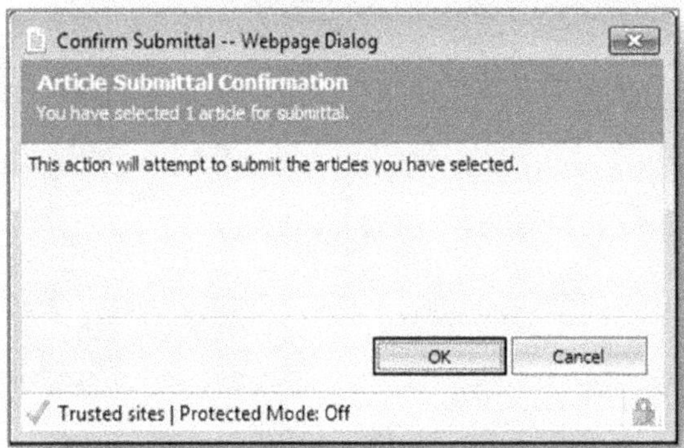

Submitting and approving knowledge base articles

You'll want to be careful about what gets published in the knowledge base. Your fellow service technicians wouldn't like it very much if you made a mistake in one of your articles. Articles initially entered into the database show in draft form.

Once you're comfortable with a knowledge base article you've written, you can submit it for approval. Articles submitted for approval can be approved, and once they're approved, they'll show up for other members of your team.

Step-by-Step Instructions

1. Click Service on the Navigation Pane, and then click Knowledge Base.

2. Click the Unapproved queue on the left.

3. Highlight an article.

4. Click Publish on the Actions toolbar.

Tips & Tricks

➢ Only certain security roles have the permission to publish knowledge base articles.

Adding comments to a knowledge base article

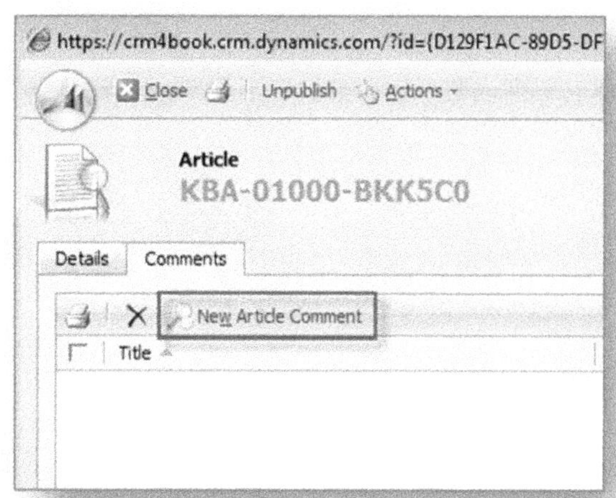

Do you have a little bit of extra information that needs to be added to the knowledge base, but doesn't actually need its own article? Is a particular article not up to date?

Have you found an alternate workaround for a process described in a knowledge base entry? All of these scenarios are perfect examples of situations where your team would benefit from adding a comment to a knowledge base article.

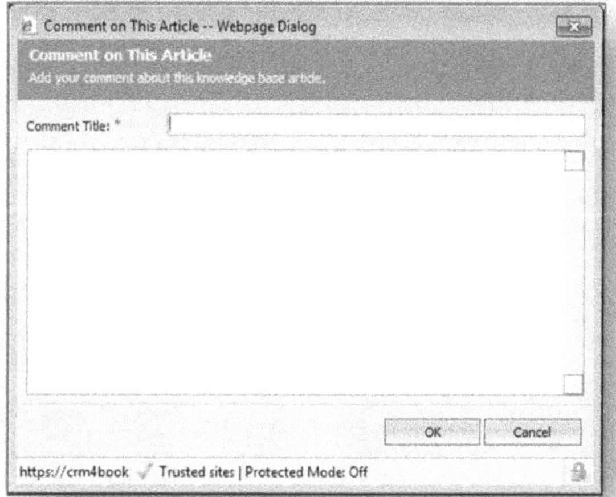

Step-by-Step Instructions

1. Open a knowledge base article.
2. Click Actions on the toolbar, then Add Article Comment.
3. Enter in your Comment and click OK.

Tips & Tricks

- If you see an error in a knowledge base article, you could add a comment if you don't have security permissions to revise the article itself.

So what did you do all week?

Running SQL Reporting Services reports ◆ Creating new reports

Running SQL Server Reporting Services reports

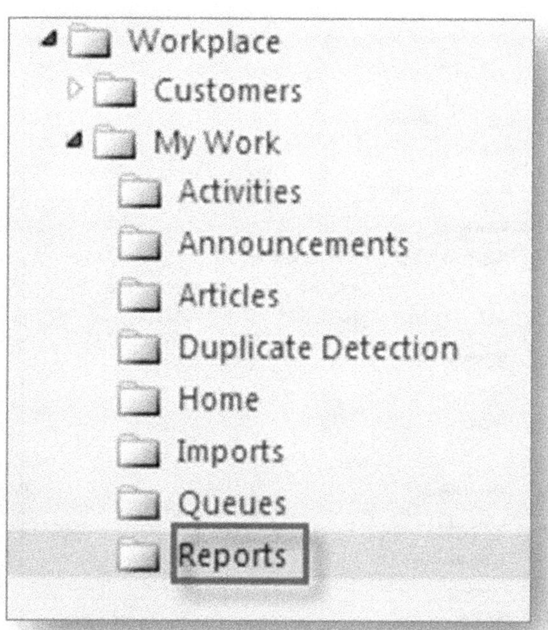

So you have a bunch of data. Now you're going to need in a report form so that you can actually understand it.

SQL Server Reporting Services (SSRS) is the reporting service built right into Microsoft Dynamics CRM, so if you want to work with reports without leaving CRM, then use SSRS reports.

CRM Online gives you a wizard that makes it easy to create SSRS reports - without the need for a programmer or staff person with report writing skills.

Step-by-Step Instructions

1. Click Workplace on the Navigation Pane, and then click Reports.
2. You can also go to a list of records and click Reports on the Actions toolbar.

Tips & Tricks

- The report writer in CRM Online isn't compatible with SSRS reports that have been created locally. This limits their usefulness, but CRM 2011 overcomes this obstacle.

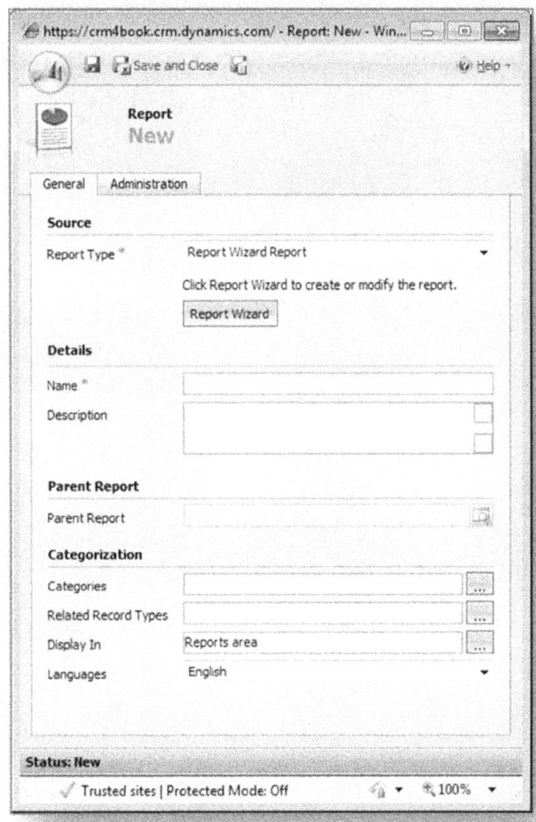

Creating new reports with the report wizard

The process of creating a report is traditionally a pretty complicated process. Fortunately you can create a report by using a simple wizard in Microsoft Dynamics CRM. All you'll need to know is what you want your report to show.

Reports created with this wizard can print to your printer, can be saved as a PDF file, or they can be saved as an editable Excel spreadsheet.

Step-by-Step Instructions

1. Click Workplace on the Navigation Pane, and then click Reports.
2. Click the New button on the Action toolbar.
3. Click the Report Wizard.
4. Start a new report and click Next.
5. Follow the instructions to create the structure of your report.

Tips & Tricks

- Instead of using the Report Wizard to create a report, consider using Excel and Pivot Tables to accomplish the same thing. You'll find that it's a lot more flexible to do the reports in Excel.

CHAPTER

22

Management needs a picture version of the reports.

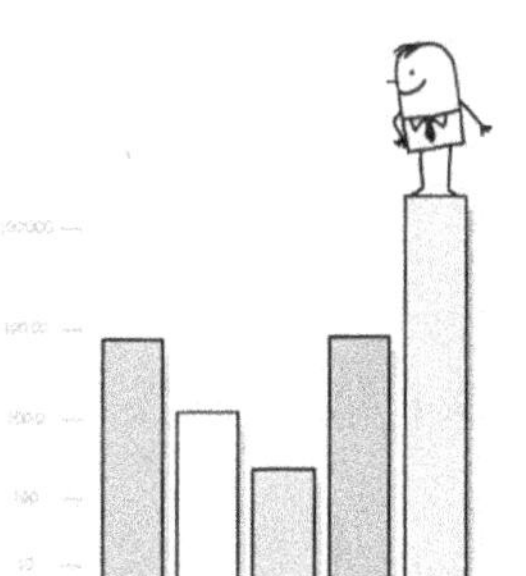

Editing the dashboard view (Home Screen) ◆ Creating custom charts ◆ Drilling down data on your dashboards

Editing the dashboard view (Home Screen)

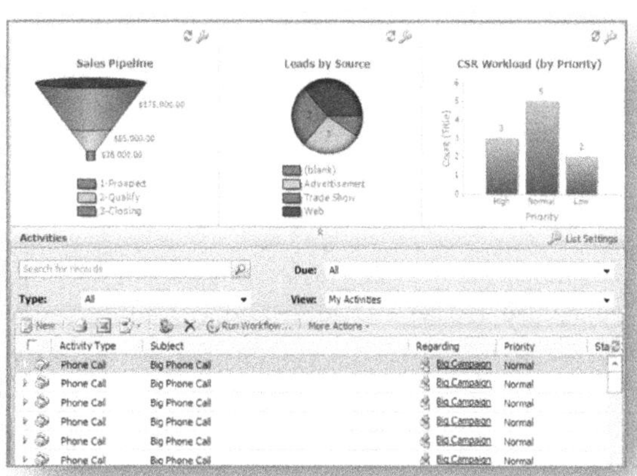

Admittedly field views aren't very attractive. Long lists of data can get pretty boring...pretty quickly. So if you are software aesthete, you might want to take a look at the dashboards on the Home Screen.

You can customize the number and type of charts that show up on your Home Screen. You can also choose which record type and default view show up in the list below your charts.

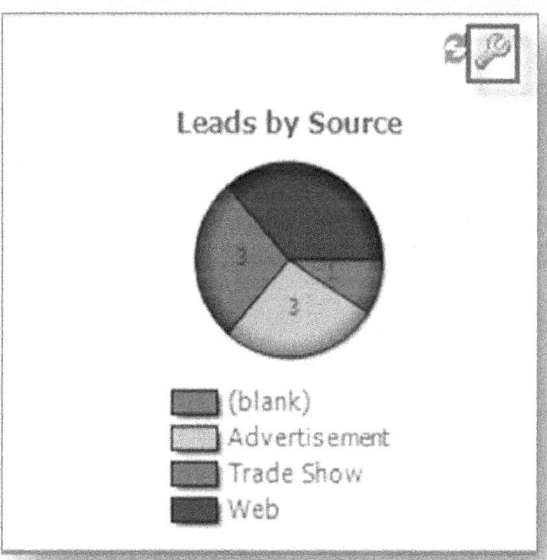

Step-by-Step Instructions

1. Click Workplace on the Navigation Pane, and then click Home.
2. Click on the wrench icon in the top-right corner of one of your charts.
3. Choose the number of charts/lists you'd like to see on the Home screen.
4. Change the chart that should show in this pane of your Home Screen.

Tips & Tricks

➢ Customize charts in Settings | Customization | Customize Entities.

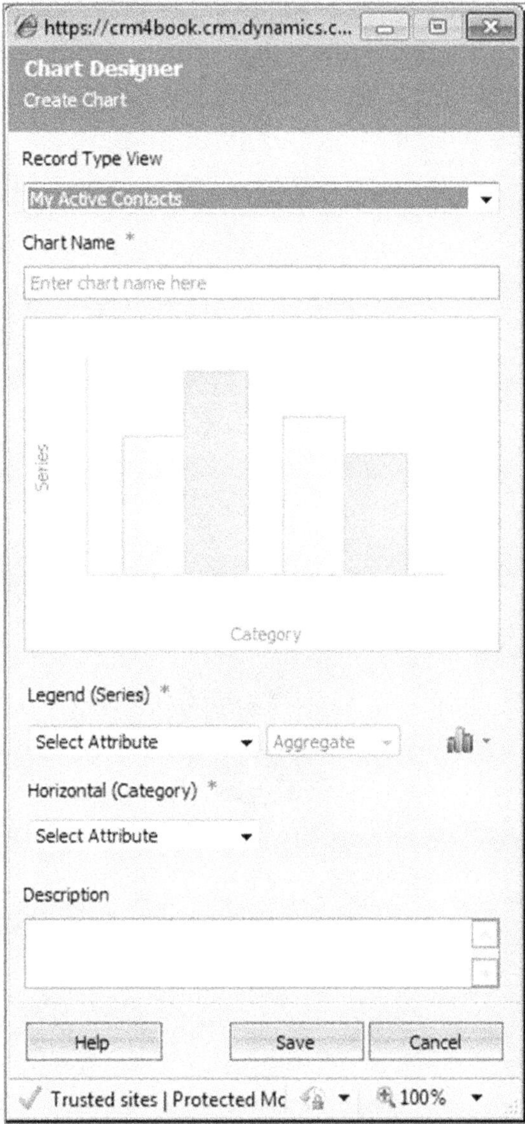

Creating custom charts

Like most things in Microsoft Dynamics CRM, the charts on your dashboard are customizable. When creating a custom chart, you can select the record type and view that your chart reports.

You can choose what shows on the X and Y axis of your bar charts, and you can change what the slices of your pie chart. Pie charts, line charts, and bar graphs can all be created.

Step-by-Step Instructions

1. Click Settings on the Navigation Pane, and then click Customization.
2. Click Customize Entities.
3. Double-click an entity.
4. Click the Charts option on the left and create a new chart for the entity you selected..

Tips & Tricks

- Line, bar, and pie charts can be created out-of-the-box. For additional dashboard options, consider linking your CRM database with SharePoint or PerformancePoint.
- You must publish customizations before new charts will be available in the Home screen.

Drilling down data on your dashboards

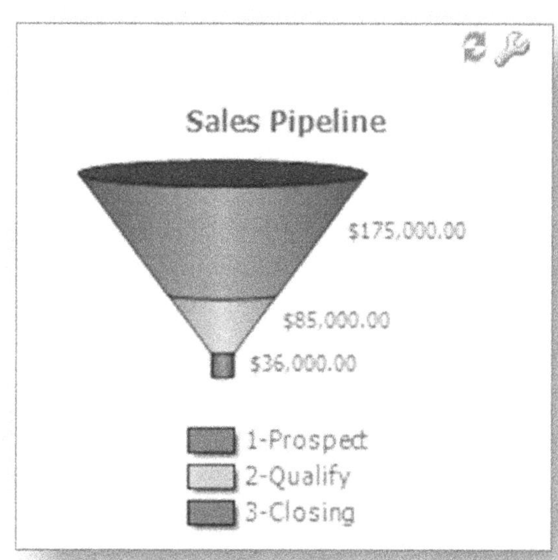

You're looking at the pie chart. It has a slice. The slice looks big. Impressive, even. But looks can be deceiving.

By drilling down into the data on your dashboard charts, you can see a specific list of the data represented in each slice of a pie or each bar in a bar graph.

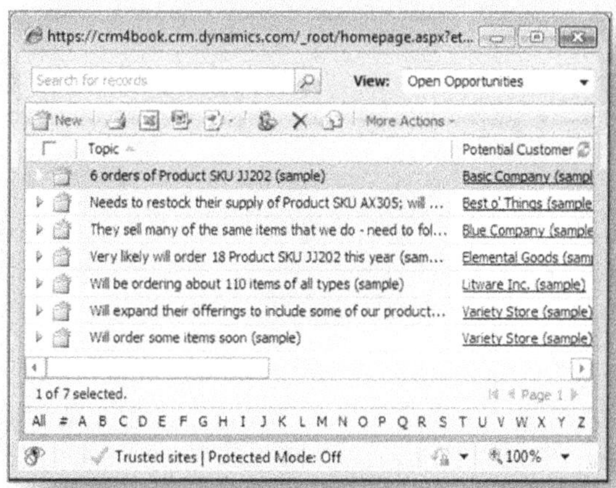

Step-by-Step Instructions

1. Click Workplace and then Home to launch your Home Screen.
2. Locate a component of one of the charts on the Home Screen. For example, you might locate one slice of a pie chart.
3. Click the slice of the pie chart. A list of data represented by that slice will appear in a list format.

Tips & Tricks

- Microsoft Dynamics CRM 2011 offers superior dashboard capabilities.

When in doubt, do it in Excel.

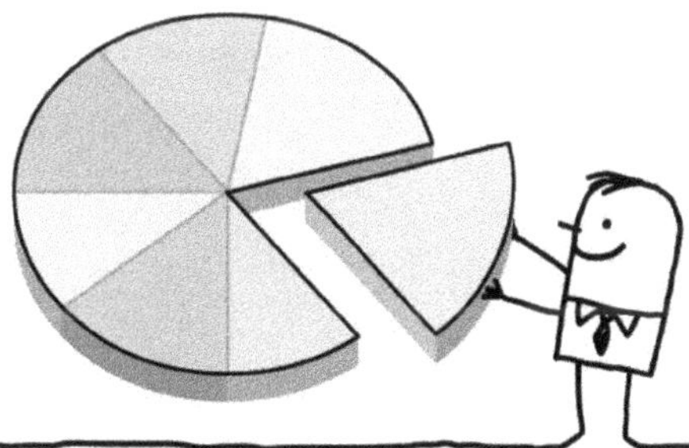

Exporting a view to Excel ◆ Exporting an Advanced Find to Excel ◆ Creating a pivot table in Excel 2003 ◆ Creating a pivot table in Excel 2007/2010

Exporting a view to Excel

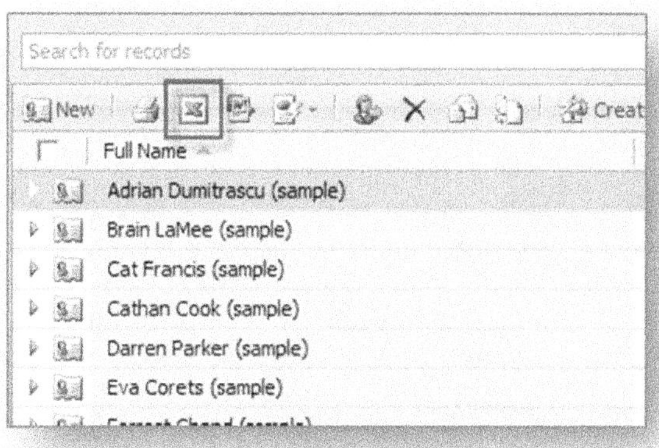

Many people prefer to use Microsoft Office Excel to make reports of their data. It can be a bit easier to analyze data if it is in spreadsheet form, and Excel is a very powerful tool for generating reports. It's certainly easier to learn Excel than it is to learn a complex report writer.

If you want to export a specific group of records to Excel, you can then create pivot tables, pie charts, bar graphs, or other complex analysis right within Excel.

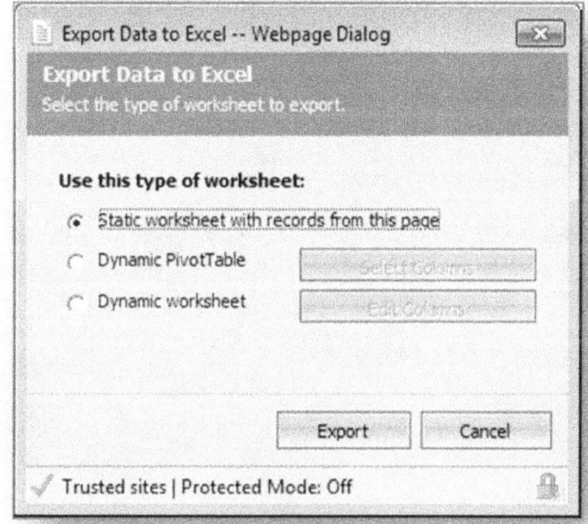

Step-by-Step Instructions

1. Go to any list of records and select a view under the view drop-down.
2. Click the Excel button on the toolbar.
3. Choose to export a static worksheet and click export.
4. Click Open.

Tips & Tricks

- Exporting a dynamic spreadsheet generally won't work in CRM Online. Dynamic exports in CRM Online require that you have offline access enabled and only pull data from your local instance of SQL, not from the live server.

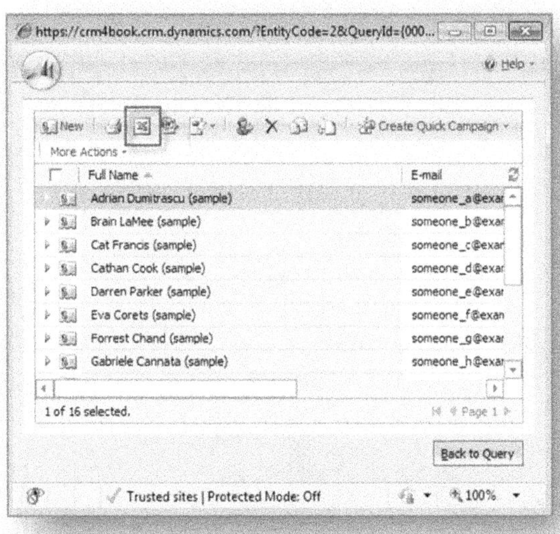

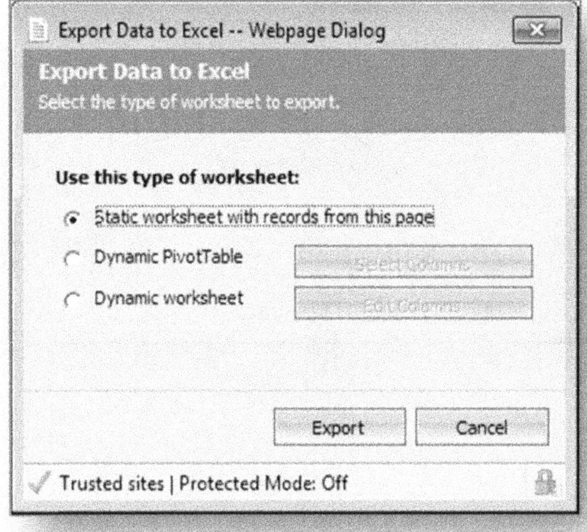

Exporting an Advanced Find to Excel

Do you have a really specific set of records that needs to be exported to Excel? By running an Advanced Find and then exporting the search results to Excel, you can limit the amount of data that gets exported to Excel.

Plus, since you can change the columns that appear in your Advanced Find, you can use this method of export to get a very specific subset of your database into Excel.

Step-by-Step Instructions

1. Run an Advanced Find
2. Click the Excel button on the toolbar.
3. Choose to export a static worksheet and click export.
4. Click Open.

Tips & Tricks

- The view that determines the default set of columns displayed when an Advanced Find is executed is called the Advanced Find view. Each entity has one, and the administrator can edit this default view in Settings | Customization | Customize Entities | Choose an entity | Forms & Views.

Creating a pivot table in Excel 2003

Flat tables can be overwhelming and hard to understand. If you want a table that will allow you to really make sense of your data, you should use a pivot table in Microsoft Office Excel. Pivot tables slice and dice the spreadsheets of CRM data that you've exported to Excel.

A plain spreadsheet might show all of your opportunities. It might show the owner, estimated revenue, and products sold on each opportunity. By running a pivot table, you can easily turn this long list of data - for example - into a summary report that shows a list of owners and the sum total of their opportunity estimated revenues.

Step-by-Step Instructions

1. Export data to Excel.
2. Save the spreadsheet. You can only run pivot tables on spreadsheets that have been saved.
3. Click Data | PivotTable and PivotChart Report.
4. Click Finish.
5. Configure your pivot table or pivot chart. For more information, go to bit.ly/pivot2003.

Creating a pivot table in Excel 2007/2010

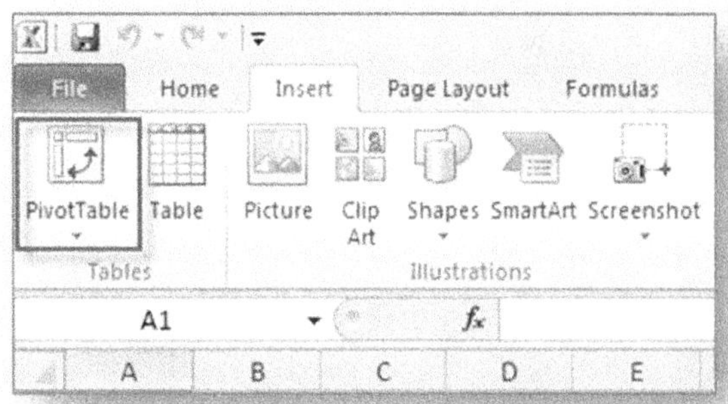

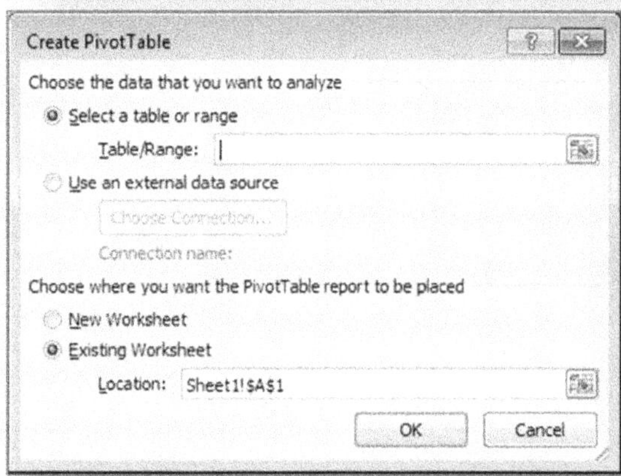

Pivot tables in Excel 2007 or 2007 follow the same basic concepts as pivot tables in Excel 2003, but the implementation of the feature is significantly different.

Step-by-Step Instructions

1. Export data to Excel.
2. Save the spreadsheet. You can only run pivot tables on spreadsheets that have been saved.
3. Click Insert on the ribbon. Click Pivot Table and choose the option to either create a pivot table or a pivot table with a pivot chart.
4. Configure your pivot table or pivot chart. For more information, go to bit.ly/pivot2007.

Tips & Tricks

- Do a Youtube or Bing search for "Pivot Tables" for some great resources and videos that will guide you through the process of creating pivot tables and pivot charts.

Adding and removing users

Adding a new user ◆ Deactivating users and reassigning data ◆ Defining security roles ◆ Buying additional licenses ◆ Creating teams of users ◆ Creating business units ◆ Changing a user's Windows Live ID ◆ Resending an invitation

Adding a new user

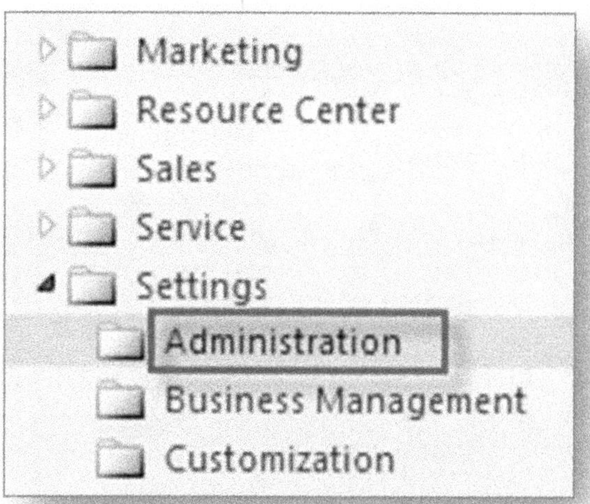

Do you want the co-worker in the next cubicle to experience the same euphoria you get from using Microsoft Dynamics CRM? Then add him or her as a new user.

Don't get ahead of yourself, though. If you don't have the licensing to do so, you can't add a new user.

Users
Add new users. Edit information about users and deactivate user records. Manage the teams, roles, and licenses assigned to users.

Step-by-Step Instructions

1. Click Settings on the Navigation Pane, and then click Administration.
2. Click Users.
3. Click the New button on the Actions toolbar.
4. Select a business unit and click Next.
5. Choose a security role and click Next.
6. Enter in information about the user and click Next.
7. Click Create New Users.

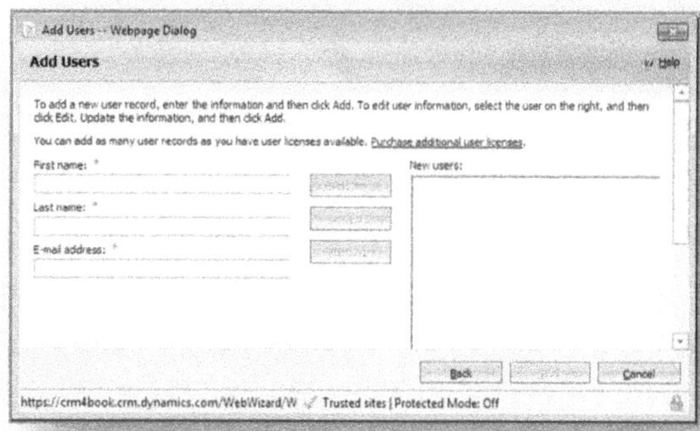

Tips & Tricks

- If a user leaves your organization, you can disable the user. Click Settings | Administration | Users. Then, highlight the user and from the More Actions drop-down, choose the Disable option.
- Disabled users can't log in, and they don't count toward the number of available licenses you've purchased.

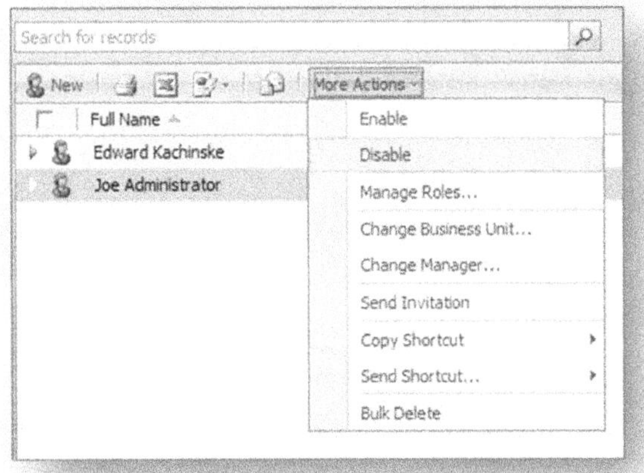

Deactivating users and reassigning data

Has a Microsoft Dynamics CRM user left your organization? Don't let that license go to waste! Deactivating a user will free up a license and the former user will no longer have access to Microsoft Dynamics CRM.

Don't worry if that former user had some important data. You can reassign the data en masse to another user. (Or you could leave it as-is.)

Step-by-Step Instructions

1. Click Settings on the Navigation Pane, and then click Administration.

2. Click Users.

3. Highlight the user that you'd like to deactivate.

4. Click the More actions button on the toolbar, the Disable.

5. Click OK.

6. Double-click the user record.

7. Click the Actions button on the toolbar, then Reassign Records.

8. Click OK.

Tips & Tricks

- In the list of users, go to the Disabled Users view to see users who have been disabled.

Defining user security roles

Everyone in your organization shouldn't be able to have the same security role. That's why it's important to set security roles for users in your database. Security roles define the level of access that a user has to the types of data and certain features in the data.

You might, for example, want to restrict some of your users' ability to delete certain types of records. This way, a user won't accidentally (or otherwise) delete all of the contacts in your database.

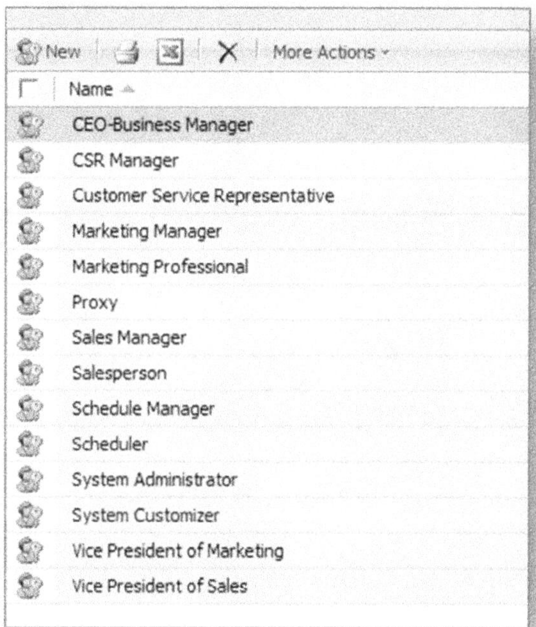

Entity	Create	Read	Write	Delete
Account	●	●	●	●
Contact	●	●	●	●
Lead	●	●	●	●
Opportunity	●	●	●	●
Activity	●	●	●	●
Note	●	●	●	●
E-mail Template	●	●	●	●
Announcement	●	●	●	●
Subject	●	●	●	●
Queue	●	●	●	●

Step-by-Step Instructions

1. Click Settings on the Navigation Pane, and then click Administration.
2. Click Security Roles.
3. Click the New button on the Actions toolbar.
4. Give the User a name.
5. Under each tab, designate the user's level of access.
6. Click Save and Close.

Tips & Tricks

- Don't start from scratch. Take a security role that is similar to the one you're creating. Highlight that role and choose Copy Role from the More Actions drop-down.

Buying additional licenses

Have you used up all of your licenses? Fear not! You can buy as many additional licenses as your budget (or credit card limit) will allow.

When you add an additional license, you won't be able to remove this license during the term of your contract without paying a penalty, so you wouldn't want to add licenses that you're not planning on using in the short term.

Step-by-Step Instructions

1. Click Settings on the Navigation Pane, and then click Administration.

2. Click Subscription Management.

3. Click Add Licenses.

Tips & Tricks

- When buying more licenses, you will be able to see your new monthly total.

- You can also add more available storage space in the Subscription Management section.

- Only the billing administrator will be able to perform this task. This is generally the person who originally set up the CRM Online subscription.

Creating teams of users

You shouldn't try to take on everything yourself. Creating a team of users will help people in your organization work more efficiently with each other

Team structures in CRM are mostly used for sharing records on a one-off basis. (You'll use business units for most of your default record sharing settings. You can share any record (or a set of records) with an individual user or a team of users.

Teams
Add new teams and new members to existing teams. Modify the team description and delete members from teams.

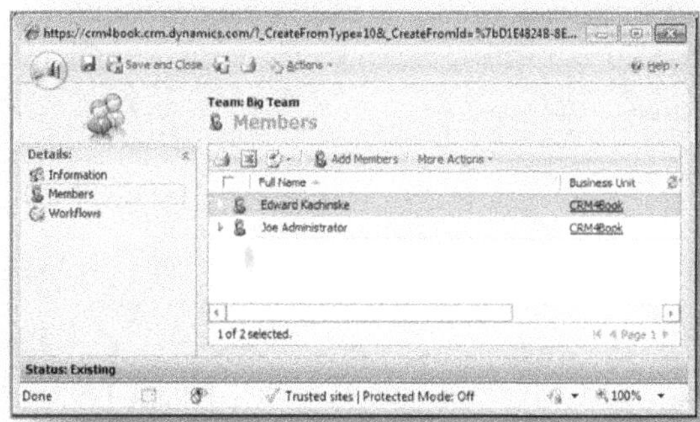

Step-by-Step Instructions

1. Click Settings on the Navigation Pane, and then click Administration.
2. Click Teams.
3. Click the New button on the Actions toolbar.
4. Give a name and business unit to your team.
5. Click Save. Go to the next page to add users.

Tips & Tricks

- To remove a user from a team, just open the user record and click the Teams option on the left.

Creating business units

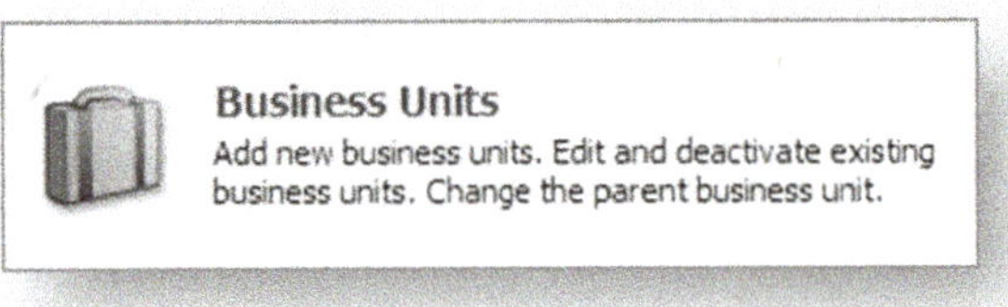

Business Units
Add new business units. Edit and deactivate existing business units. Change the parent business unit.

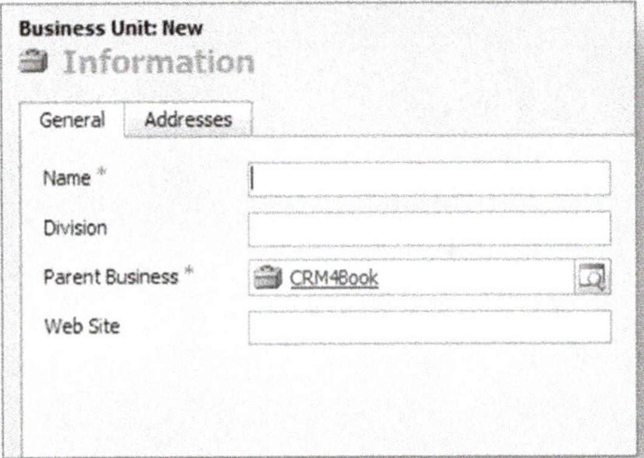

Microsoft Dynamics CRM allows you to organize your company under different business units. You might set up business units for each individual operating unit within your company, but even if your company is small, you might also set up business units for each team or functional role within the business.

When you are creating a security role, which will determine what level of access each user has to parts of the database, one of the things you'll be able to do is restrict access to just records owned within your business unit. So, if you're in the East Coast business unit, you might only see records owned by other people in the East Coast business unit.

Step-by-Step Instructions

1. Click Settings on the Navigation Pane, and then click Administration.

2. Click Business Units.

3. Click the New button on the Actions toolbar.

4. Give the business unit a name.

5. Click Save and Close.

Tips & Tricks

- Users must belong to one (and only one) business unit.
- Business units cannot be deleted.

Changing a user's Windows Live ID

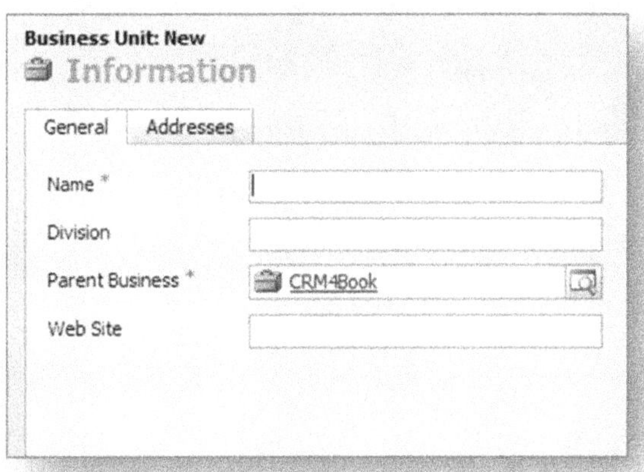

The Windows Live ID is the primary login mechanism for CRM Online, and you can get one for free. When you set up a user, the system will assume that this user's Windows Live ID is the same as the e-mail address that you specified when you configured the user's account.

Sometimes, though, you may need to change the Windows Live ID for a user. For example, if your organization changes domain names and your users change e-mail addresses, you'd have to change both the e-mail address *and* the Windows Live ID for your users.

Step-by-Step Instructions

1. Click Settings on the Navigation Pane, and then click Administration.
2. Click Users.
3. Double-click a user record.
4. Click Actions on the toolbar, then Change Windows Live ID.

Tips & Tricks

- If your users are also Hotmail users, you might want to change their WLID's to their Hotmail address. This will reduce the number of sign in/sign out frustrations they experience.

Resending an invitation

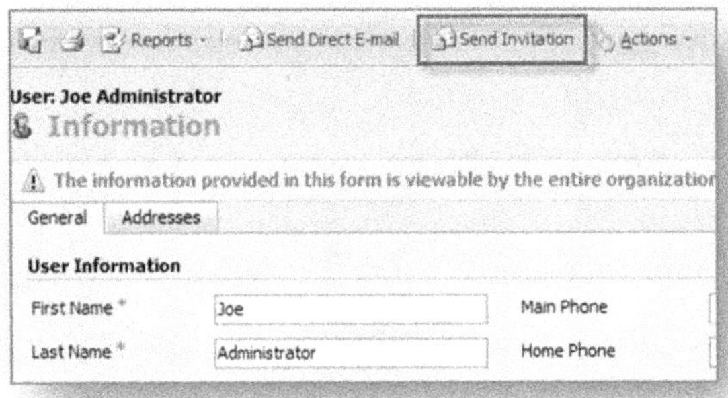

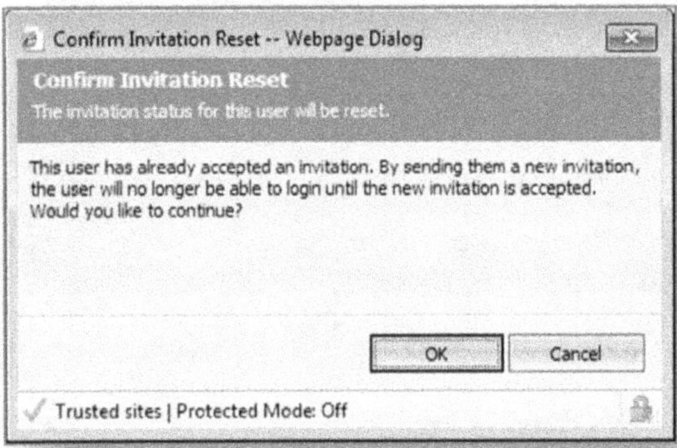

When you add a new user, you have to send an invitation to this user before he/she can login. The invitation comes in the form of an e-mail to the user.

Invitations are only valid for three days, so sometimes they need to be resent. If you set up a user recently, and the user isn't able to log in, it's likely that you will need to resend the invitation.

Step-by-Step Instructions

1. Click Settings on the Navigation Pane, and then click Administration.
2. Click Users.
3. Double-click a user record.
4. Click Resend Invitation on the toolbar.

Tips & Tricks

- If the invitation emails are getting caught in your spam filters, send the invitation again and just try logging into the database (in Internet Explorer) as the user. You'll be prompted to accept the terms of use, and the system should grant your new user access to the database from that point forward.

Workflow is easier than doing it by hand

Creating a new Workflow ◆ Adding Workflow steps ◆ Publishing a Workflow ◆ Workflow example: Creating a follow up task for new opportunities

Creating a new Workflow

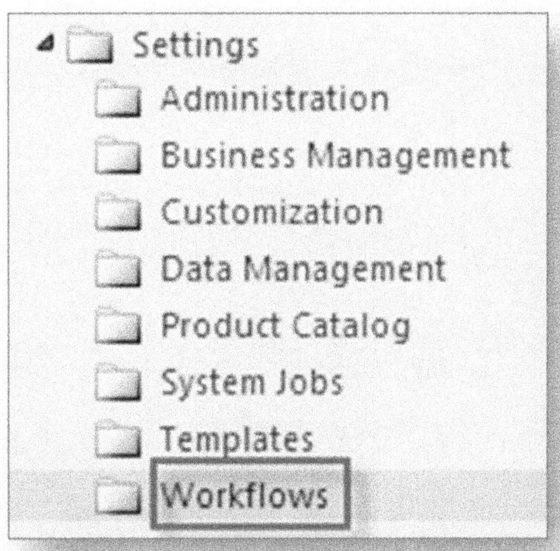

Workflows are like macros on steroids. A workflow can perform automated tasks, either on-demand or because some condition has been met within the database.

So, when a new opportunity is entered into the system, workflow could see that a new record has been created, and it might invoke and automatically create a follow-up task in a week and send an e-mail back to the customer thanking him/her for the opportunity to do business.

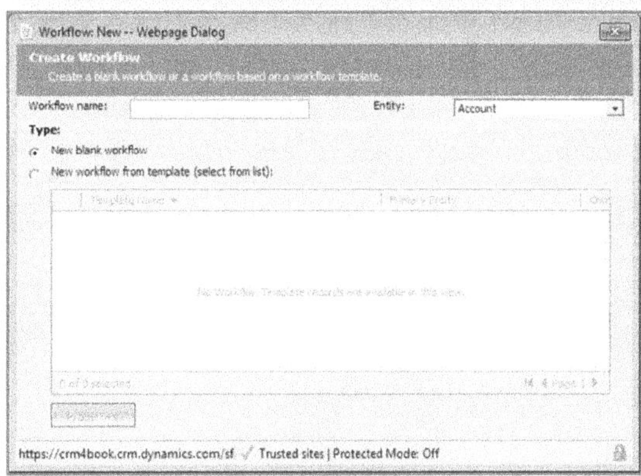

Step-by-Step Instructions

1. Click Settings on the Navigation Pane, and then click Workflows.
2. Click the New button on the Actions toolbar.
3. Give your workflow a name and choose the type of entity that the workflow will work with.
4. Click OK. The workflow will appear and will be ready to add steps.

Tips & Tricks

- When creating a workflow, you need to specify whether the workflow will run just for yourself, for your business unit, or for the entire organization.
- You'll also need to specify whether the workflow will engage on-demand or when an action occurs in the database.

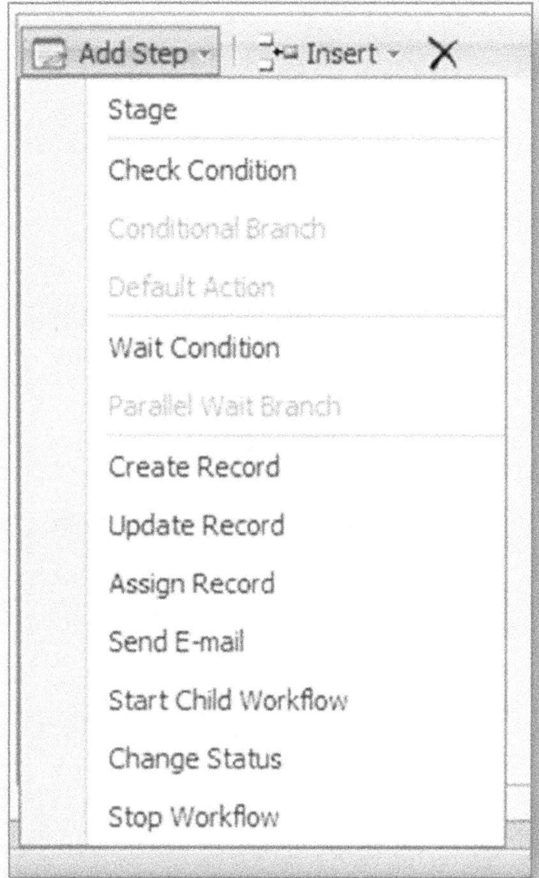

Adding Workflow steps

A workflow can be made of multiple steps. The steps could wait for something to happen, they could check for a condition within the database. Workflow can also create new records, like contacts or tasks in Outlook.

One of the workflow steps can even kill the workflow. The sum total of all of the steps in your workflow is the task that will be performed when the workflow is invoked.

Step-by-Step Instructions

1. Open an unpublished workflow.
2. In the steps area of the workflow, click the Add Step button. Choose the type of step you'd like to add.
3. Depending on the type of step you're adding, you'll have to clarify details for the step. You can add as many steps as you require. Workflow will perform each step in order.

Tips & Tricks

- You cannot update a picklist field through workflow.
- Types of steps available in Workflow are: Check Condition, Wait Condition, Create Record, Update Record, Assign Record, Send E-mail, Start Child Workflow, Change Status, and End Workflow.

Publishing a Workflow

When you create a workflow, the workflow is saved in a draft mode. It won't actually become available until you publish it.

This gives you a chance to work on the details of the workflow before you deploy it to the entire database. You'll want to have the option to keep a workflow in a draft form, since workflows can perform tasks that modify (and possibly destroy) the data in your system.

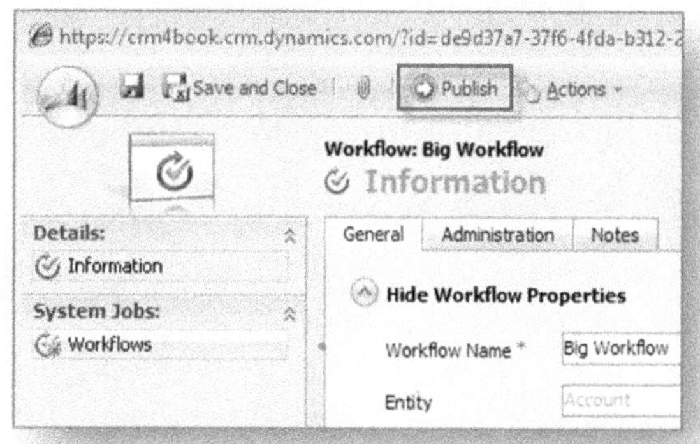

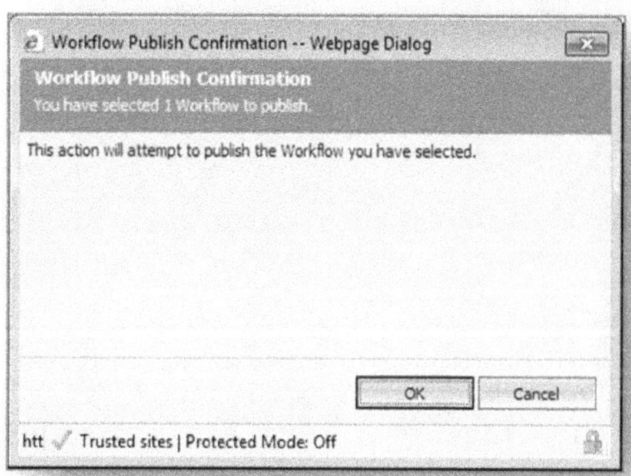

Step-by-Step Instructions

1. Click Settings on the Navigation Pane, and then click Workflows.
2. Highlight the workflow you'd like to publish.
3. Click the Publish button on the Actions toolbar.

Tips & Tricks

- You can only publish workflows that you own.
- Click the Assign button on the Actions toolbar to assign a workflow to yourself if you don't have access to edit or publish a specific workflow.

Workflow example: creating a follow-up task for new opportunities

In this example, we'll walk through the steps required to set Microsoft Dynamics CRM to automatically create a follow-up task whenever an opportunity is entered into the system.

Step-by-Step Instructions

1. Create a new workflow on the opportunity entity.

2. In the Options for Automatic Workflows area, choose Organization for the scope. The workflow will engage for all users.

3. In the Start When area, the only thing that should be checked is the Record is created option. This way, the workflow will only engage when a new opportunity is created.

4. Click the Add Step button on the toolbar and choose Create Record.

5. In the Create field, choose Task.

6. Click the Set Properties and configure how you'd like this automatic task to look in Outlook.

7. Click the Save button on the toolbar and then Publish.

Tailoring the system to meet your needs

Adding new fields ◆ Modifying the default views ◆ Modifying the forms ◆ Creating custom entities ◆ Publishing customizations

Adding new fields

Don't like the way Microsoft Dynamics looks "out-of-the-box?' Do you want different fields to show up in a record view? Buying Microsoft Dynamics CRM is kind of like buying a house. It's a great framework, but it doesn't become a home until you configure the furniture.

Fortunately, you can easily add new fields to any record view. Customization in Microsoft Dynamics CRM is easy, and in no time you'll have the database looking the way you want it to.

Step-by-Step Instructions

1. Click Settings on the Navigation Pane, and then click Customization.
2. Click Customize Entities.
3. Double-click an entity.
4. Click Forms and Views on the left, then double-click Form.
5. Click Add Fields under Common Tasks to add a field.
6. Select the field you want to add, then designate a tab and a section. Click OK.
7. Click Save and Close. Remember to publish your customizations.

Tips & Tricks

- Click the Save and New button instead of Save and Close if you are adding multiple fields.

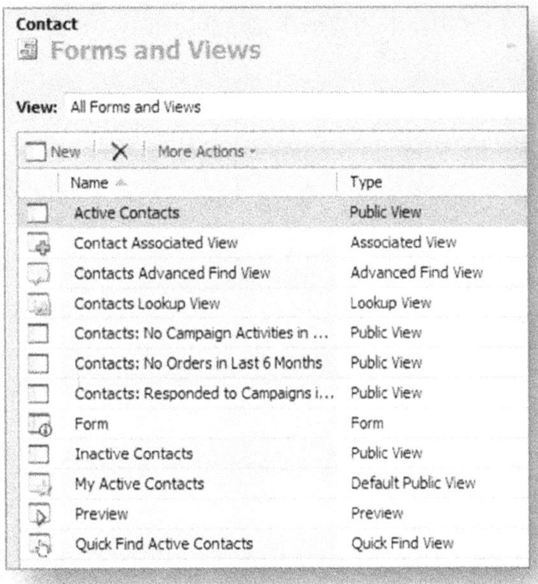

Modifying the default views

Whenever you look at a list of records, you're looking at a view. Go to the contacts screen in CRM, and in the upper right corner of the list of records, check out the View drop-down. This drop-down will show you the current view of records.

You might not like the way a certain view looks. You might, for example, want to add or remove the columns that show up in your Active Contacts view. Modifying the default views is easy and similar to any other entity customization that you might do in Microsoft Dynamics CRM.

Step-by-Step Instructions

1. Click Settings on the Navigation Pane, and then click Customization.
2. Click Customize Entities.
3. Double-click an entity.
4. Click Forms and Views on the left, then double-click a view, such as Active Accounts.
5. Click Add Columns under Common Tasks to add a column. Click OK.
6. Select a column by clicking on it. You can change its position with the arrow buttons under Common Tasks.
7. Select a column and click Remove under Common Tasks to remove it.

Modifying the forms

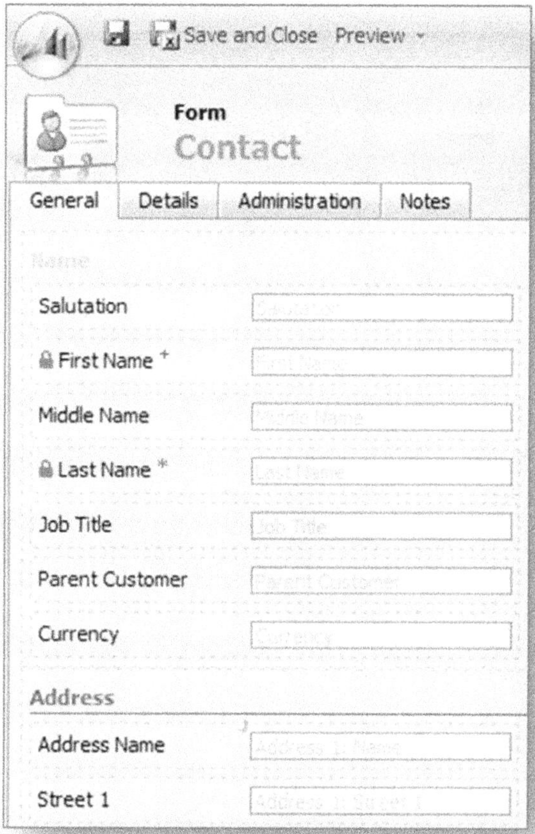

When you open a record in Microsoft Dynamics CRM, the screen that lets you edit the record is called the form.

Forms in Microsoft Dynamics CRM are highly customizable. You can add fields, tabs, and sections to your record view. You can also move things around so everything looks the way you want it to.

Step-by-Step Instructions

1. Click Settings on the Navigation Pane, and then click Customization.
2. Click Customize Entities.
3. Double-click an entity.
4. Click Forms and Views on the left, then double-click Form.

Tips & Tricks

- Click the Form Properties option to add custom javascript code to your forms.
- There is one form for all users. Changes made to the form will appear on everyone's system.

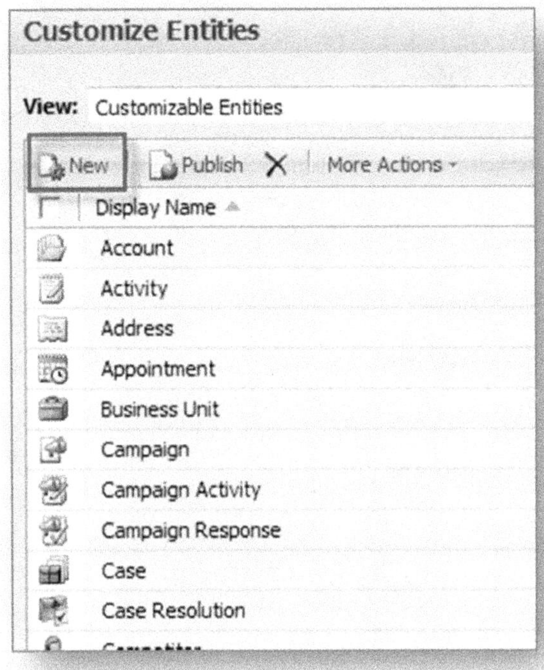

Creating custom entities

Types of records in Microsoft Dynamics CRM are called entities. Contacts, accounts, tasks, sales literature, and opportunities are all examples of entities that exist with an out-of-the-box CRM database.

Your organization might want to keep track of an entity that doesn't with Microsoft Dynamics CRM. Don't worry, though, because it's really easy to create custom entities in Microsoft Dynamics CRM.

Step-by-Step Instructions

1. Click Settings on the Navigation Pane, and then click Customization.

2. Click Customize Entities.

3. Click New.

4. Enter in information about your entity and click Save and Close.

Tips & Tricks

➢ You can also change the name of any existing entity. For example, you might change Accounts to Companies. In the list of entities, just double-click an entity and you'll have the option to change its name.

➢ No entity changes will be made until you publish. From the list of entities, click More Actions | Publish All Customizations.

Publishing customizations

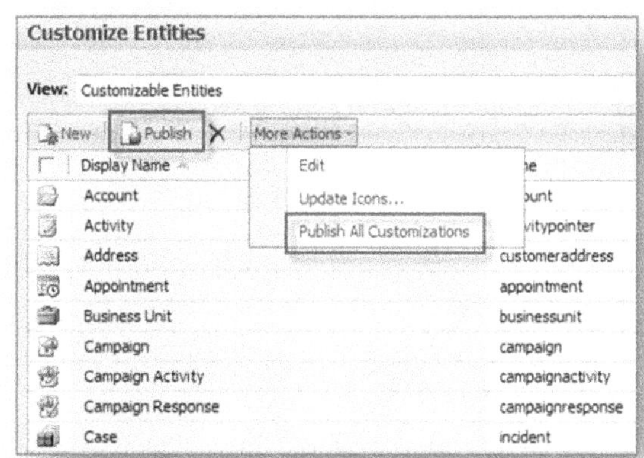

Hold it right there. Just because you've done a customization doesn't mean that it will show up in your database.

No changes that you make to the database will show up until you publish your customizations.

Step-by-Step Instructions

1. Click Settings on the Navigation Pane, and then click Customization.
2. Click Customize Entities.
3. Click More Actions on the toolbar, then Publish All Customizations.

Tips & Tricks

- You can export a backup of your customizations at any time. Click Settings | Customization | Export Customizations.
- You can then import customizations by clicking Settings | Customization | Import Customizations.

CHAPTER 27

Setting Preferences

Setting the default startup screen ◆ Setting the default number of records shown per page ◆ Turning off the e-mail tracking token

Setting the default startup screen

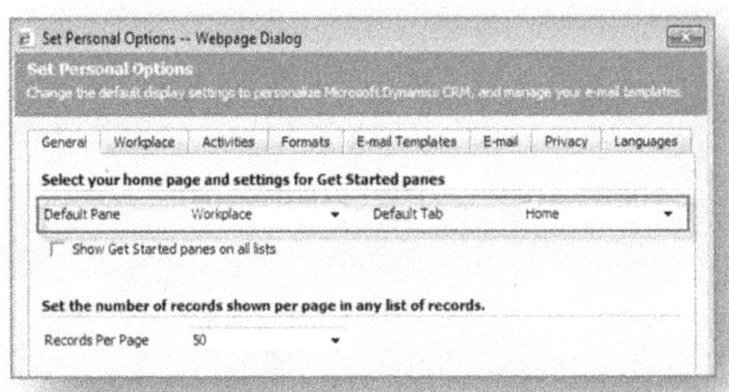

If you are a service technician, you probably want the Cases screen to pop up when you first open Microsoft Dynamics CRM. If you are a salesperson, it might be useful to have the system automatically open to your list of open opportunities.

You can change the default startup screen in Microsoft Dynamics CRM. Both the default pane and tab can be set.

Step-by-Step Instructions

1. On the main screen, click Tools on the toolbar. (Or CRM | Options if you're in Outlook.)
2. Click Options.
3. Select the default pane and tab.

Tips & Tricks

- Each user has his/her own default startup screen.
- This applies to CRM users who use Internet Explorer to log in. Outlook users can ignore this page.

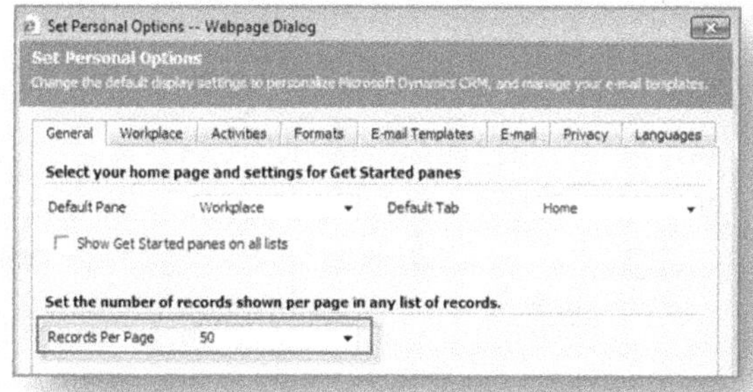

Setting the default number of records show per page

Is that big list of records a bit overwhelming? Or are you a data fiend who wants even more records to show up on one page? Either way, you're in luck.

Microsoft Dynamics CRM lets you set the default number of records that show up on a page. The default is 50, but most users find it more useful to show 250 records per page.

Step-by-Step Instructions

1. On the main screen, click Tools on the toolbar. (Or CRM | Options if you are in Outlook.)
2. Click Options.
3. Under the General Tab, set the default number of records.

Tips & Tricks

- There is no way to view more than 250 records per page on any CRM entity.
- If you need to see more than 250 records at a time, export to Excel and analyze your data in Excel.

Turning off the e-mail tracking token

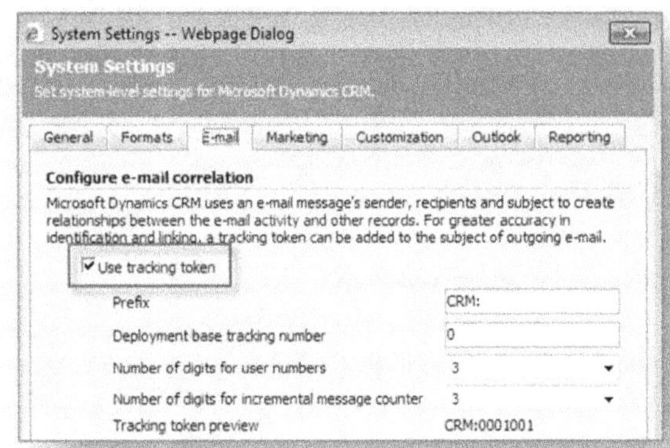

If you've sent e-mail that is tracked in the CRM database, you've probably noticed that CRM appends a long string of numbers to the end of outgoing e-mail messages.

This string of text is called the tracking token and looks something like this: CRM:001002034. If a customer responds to this e-mail and leaves the tracking token intact, then the response from the customer is also tracked in CRM.

Many customers don't like the looks of the tracking token, and turning it off only removes the automatic tracking of responses.

Step-by-Step Instructions

1. Click Settings on the Navigation Pane, and then click Administration.
2. Click System Settings.
3. Click the E-mail tab.
4. Uncheck the Use tracking token option.

Tips & Tricks

- If you decide to use the e-mail tracking token, you can change the format of the token by clicking Settings | Administration | Auto-Numbering.

www.ingramcontent.com/pod-product-compliance
Lightning Source LLC
Chambersburg PA
CBHW080410060326
40689CB00019B/4193

* 9 7 8 1 4 6 3 5 4 1 1 7 0 *